SPIRAL GUIDE

SARDINIA

C000052028

AA
Publishing

Contents

Written by Adele Evans

Verified by Mary McLean

Project editor Edith Summerhayes
Copy edited by Stephanie Smith
Designer Catherine Murray
Cartographic editor Anna Thompson

Published by AA Publishing, a trading name of Automobile
Association Developments Limited, whose registered office is
Fanum House, Basing View, Basingstoke, Hampshire, RG21 4EA.
Registered number 1878835.

ISBN: 978-0-7495-5714-0

A CIP catalogue record for this book is available from the
British Library.

Cover design and binding style by permission of AA Publishing

Colour separation by Keenes, Andover
Printed and bound in China by Leo Paper Products

Find out more about AA Publishing and the wide range of services
the AA provides by visiting our website at www.theAA.com/travel

A03011
Maps in this title produced from mapping © Freytag-Berndt u.
Artaria KG, 1231 Vienna-Austria

the magazine

La Sardità

Cast away in the middle of the Mediterranean, the Italian island of Sardinia is often nicknamed "the small continent". The second largest island after Sicily has idyllic ivory beaches lapped by silky waters in every shade of blue. Yet inland you will find a traditional land of shepherds, of wild landscape sprinkled with archaeological sites, rolling hills and meadows bright with wild flowers – a Mediterranean Eden full of contrasts and seductive charm.

The coastline of almost 2,000km (1,250 miles) is indented by tiny coves, picturesque harbours and rugged cliffs. It is a quarter of the total Italian coast and has Italy's best beaches, lapped by clear seas. Paradoxically, for the Sardinians traditionally the sea was synonymous with those who came to plunder – "*furat chi beit dae su mare*" ("he who comes from the sea comes to rob"). Phoenicians, Romans, Arabs, Catalans and mainland Italians have all left their mark, but the unique prehistoric stone towers, *nuraghi*, bear testament to the Sardinians' long history of independence – and their *Sardità*, or Sardness.

The Sard language is mostly based on Latin, but not without smatterings surviving from the Nuraghic period, such as the word *nuraghe* itself. Other words bear Phoenician, Arabic, Corsican, Genoese or Catalan among many other linguistic traces. Yet, still widely spoken and with countless different dialects, Sardinian coexists happily with Italian, which is spoken by just about everyone.

Island Pride

The Sardinians are noted for their quiet strength, indepen-dence, fierce loyalty, bravery, deep-hearted friendliness, great hospitality and, at

Page 5: The beach at La Pelosa at the northwest tip of the island
Above: Decorated float at the festival of Sant'Efisio

times, their reserve. But they know how to party too, and no other folkloric tradition in Europe survives so completely as in Sardinia. Fabulous festivals, gusty flavours and feasting and not a little magic interwoven with traditional stories of fairies and giants are all part of *la Sardita*.

The unspoiled landscape of the interior is mountainous, rugged and covered with a thick mantle of *macchia mediterranea* (Mediterranean maquis) – a highly scented tangled array of lavender, rosemary, wild fennel, herbs, and plants such as juniper, myrtle and strawberry tree. Plants unknown to the mainland thrive here and the phrase "sardonic grin" comes from the grimace found on victims of those poisoned by a certain herb found in Sardinia, which contains strychnine-like alkaloids. When eaten it induces convulsive laughter which can end in death.

Long Life and Happiness

The traditional Sard greeting "*A Kent'Annos*" ("May you live to 100") is no mere jest. Sardinia has the world's highest percentage of people past their 100th birthday; around 135 people per million live to celebrate it, while the western average is nearer 75. The fresh local food, excellent red wine, sparkling seas and infectious Sard celebratory spirit all combine to make this the Eden of the Mediterranean.

Below: The rocky wilderness of Valle della Luna, near Ággius
Bottom: Ísola Caprera

Creation Story

A Sard legend says that after completing his creation of the rest of the world, God had some rocks remaining. He decided to drop them in the Mediterranean. He surveyed his handiwork and removed a little of the best from here and there, which he sprinkled liberally over the island that became Sardinia. Many would say that he left the best until last and that this island of breathtaking beauty was his masterpiece.

Nuraghi

GIANTS' TOMBS and *fairy houses*

On hillocks cloaked with olive groves, scented with myrtle and fennel, circular stone ruins rise up – unique prehistoric rock villages built by the Nuraghic civilisation. The tombs of the Nuraghic tribal chiefs were known as "giants' tombs" (*tombe dei giganti*), while the "fairy houses" (*domus de janas*) carved into the hillside and rock faces pre-date them, going back into the mists of time.

Around 3000BC it was believed that life continued after death, so people placed food and household items in the *domus de janas*, of which about a thousand survive in Sardinia. Local superstition held that the *janas* – or fairies – who lived in these rock tombs could also be witches and had to be appeased. The walls of the tombs were often decorated with magic symbols such as horns, bulls' heads and various geometric patterns.

Shrouded in Mystery

There's a popular Sard saying that roughly translates as "A modern builder guarantees his work for five years, but the Nuraghic builder guaranteed his for 5,000." As yet they haven't lasted quite that long, but some of the 7,000 conical structures to be found in every corner of the island have been standing since 1800BC. The people who built the *nuraghi* left no written records, so almost nothing is known about their way of life, or what happened to them. In spite of fertile imaginations, the jury is still out as to whether they were originally built as homes, fortresses or tombs.

The word *nuraghi* (singular *nuraghe*) derives from *nurra*, meaning both mound and cavity. They were built by laying big stones of similar size on top of each other leaving a cavity in the middle, which was then

Cone-shaped tower at Nuraghe Losa

covered by a stone domed roof. No mortar or any kind or binding material was used between the dry stones. The Phoenician, Roman and Byzantine invaders, delighted to find such sturdy structures in situ, extended them for their own use and built settlements around them. The largest and most impressive example is Nuraghe Su Nuraxi (► 50), north of Cágliari.

Sacred Wells

The Nuraghic civilisation also worshipped the cult of water and built underground stone chambers to house sacred wells. There are about 40 of these wells remaining in Sardinia, each formed by a circular room with a small skylight and a terrace that slopes down to the fertilising water spring. Intricately crafted bronze figurines, *bronzetti*, were given as offerings to the gods as part of the cult ritual.

Superhuman Graves

Just as impressive are the Nuraghic graves, known by the locals as *tombe dei giganti*. The long burial chamber and huge blocks of granite over the entrances do indeed suggest superhuman dimensions, where, so legend says, giants are buried. The rather more matter-of-fact explanation is that they were used and reused by all members of the tribes. On the other hand, the huge slabs of stone surrounding the tombs may make you wonder who but giants could have put them there.

Below: Inside the central tower at Nuraghe Su Nuraxi

Below: View over the extensive remains at Su Nuraxi

Life is a beach

Sardinia has the most beautiful coastline in the whole of Italy and some of the world's most idyllic beaches. Mile upon mile of blonde sands dip into waters of dazzling shades of aquamarine and emerald green. Elsewhere, rugged cliffs plunge into the sea and tiny coves and picturesque harbours beg to be explored. Many of the unpolluted waters really are as blue and as clear as a swimming pool – and the sandy coves are often deserted.

For many the Costa Smeralda – Emerald Coast – is the reason that Sardinia is famous. In the 1950s, while yachting in the northeast of the island, the fabulously wealthy Prince Karim Aga Khan IV and his chums became spellbound by the translucent emerald-green waters and romantic little coves. He found a group of businessmen to join him in developing it as a resort that would protect its natural beauty, and so the Costa Smeralda was born. Those jewel colours take on every hue from sapphire blue to sparkling turquoise, so dazzling in contrast with the sugar-white sands that you can't help but sport the Prada shades. And yet, this is only a tiny area of the island's magnificent wealth of beaches.

Secret Coves

Great swathes of the Sardinian coast remain uninhabited, with pines, juniper and prickly pears encircling occasional sandy beaches, sea and granite rocks – just as the Costa Smeralda once was. Whether you go north, south, east or west, each area of coast has its own gems. Some are accessed only by little paths surrounded by

The turquoise waters of Báia Sardinia

Secluded beach on the Costa Smeralda

junipers, pine trees, oleander and eucalyptus, others by boat, but most are easily accessible with a little adventurous spirit.

Laid Back and Gorgeous

On the west coast, dunes soar and surfers carve their creamy wakes, while at the island's northwestern point white sands shelve into the most brilliant turquoise sea at La Pelosa. The pretty north-eastern resorts of Palau, Santa Teresa di Gallura, Báia Sardinia and Cannigione might lack the glamour and exclusivity of the Costa Smeralda but many prefer their laid-back feel, and all have beautiful beaches, such as the romanti-cally gorgeous Cala Luna. The east has one of Europe's last coastal forests growing right down to a seafront studded with grottos and spectacular beaches in the Golfo di Orosei. And in the south, emerald-cobalt water laps pinkish-white sand in the Báia Chia, known as the "Pearl of the South".

All of Sardinia's beaches are open to everyone. And, while it may be absurd to suggest that anyone could ever tire of the land which gave us Verdi, Vesuvius and Versace, those mainland Italians who want a change of scenery for their summer breaks come to Sardinia in their droves. Yet, even in August, only the main town beaches get crowded. While many UK (and English-speaking) visitors like the privacy and space of the quiet coves, Italians like to parade up and down on the more sociable town beaches.

Follow the Sandal

Legend says that God created Sardinia by stepping on it with his sandal. "Sandalyon" (sandal) was the ancient name given to it by the Greeks and Phoenicians.

Festivals
and country ways

The island frequently bursts into life and colour as festival time comes around again. Shrill music fills the air along with aromas of sweets, bread, herbs, cheeses and wine. If you feel it tugging at your wilder instincts, don't be surprised. Sardinia was born out of rugged traditions and jealously guards its pride as a nation of big festivals.

The festivals are usually religious in origin, but other Sardinian *feste* celebrate annual events such as the harvest or turning of the seasons, giving them a distinctly more pagan orientation. *Carnevale* (literally "farewell to meat"), usually celebrated in February, sees masked characters such as the *mamuthones* of Mamoiada in the Barbágia enacting battles between devils and animals accompanied by wild dancing, music and, of course, feasting. In picturesque little Bosa, the Carnevale celebrations have lusty, if not blatantly open, sexual connotations.

But the island's biggest festival is the religious *Sagra di Sant'Efisio* in Cágliari. On 1 May the patron saint's image is carried high on a cart drawn by decorated oxen from the capital to Nora, where Sant'Efisio was executed. It returns on the night of 4 May accompanied by throngs of people dressed in traditional costume and by the music of the *launeddas*. Unique to Sardinia, this musical instrument has three pipes made from reed that are played by musicians using their cheeks as a "wind bag". Their shrill sound accompanies many of the island's festivals.

Sássari
Perhaps competing with the capital, the second city, Sássari, has two major festivals of its own.

On the penultimate Sunday in May, the *Cavalcata Sarda*, hundreds of Sardinians in traditional costumes parade through the city centre to celebrate a victory over the Saracens in AD1000. In the afternoon there are

Parading through Cágliari for Sant'Efisio

thrilling horse races through the streets, followed by an evening of dancing and merrymaking. *I Candelieri* (The Candlesticks) takes place on 14 August, when giant wooden candlesticks are paraded through Sássari's streets in honour of the Virgin Mary.

Núoro and Cábras

In late August the mountainous interior celebrates with a spectacularly colourful parade in Núoro with the *Festa del Redentore* (Christ the Redeemer). Spread over several days of parades, music, dancing and firework displays, the festival culminates in a procession to the statue of Il Redentore on Monte Ortobene. And in September, the *Festa di San Salvatore* is celebrated by the local young men running barefoot from Cábras to the sanctuary of San Salvatore.

Throughout the year there are also many gastronomic festivals – or *sagri* – as local delicacies come into season.

Among many others, the sea urchin festival takes place in Alghero in January, the *Sagra dell'Agrume* – citrus festival – in Muravera and the *Sagra delle Castagne* (Feast of Chestnuts) fills the streets of Aritzo in October.

See page 40 for list of main festivals.

Colourful costumes are part of most festivals

THE WILD WEST

The Sards are among Italy's finest riders and especially in the "Wild West" of Oristano province. They have a special affinity with horses and often ride pure-blooded fast Arab steeds and are keen to show off their skills in spectacular – even cavalier – festivals at breakneck speed. For more relaxing forays, Oristano is well equipped with riding excursions and courses. Ala Birdi, near Arboréa, has excellent riding facilities for all levels and ages (tel: 0783 80500; www.alabirdi.it).

Sa Sartiglia

There are many festivals throughout the year in this area but two are especially remarkable. One of Sardinia's liveliest is Sa Sartiglia, held in Oristano at Carnival time. The normally staid town erupts into a frenzy of colourful costumes and thundering hooves over the two-day event. The origins go back to old tournaments, when knights on their galloping steeds had to put their lances through a ring suspended from a rope. The leader, known as *su compin-odori*, is chosen by members of the trade guilds and is the King of the Sartiglia. He is clothed and masked by young girls, *sas massaiedas*, who are supposedly virgins – at least for the duration of the festival. In white mask, black top hat and white shawl, he is carried to his elaborately costumed waiting horse. He blesses the crowd with a sceptre decorated with violets. After much parading, the competition begins in earnest when the *compinodori* gallops towards a six-pointed star hanging from a rope and tries to pierce it with his sword. Two other knights follow and the more stars that are successfully pierced, the better will be the harvest. The final ritual is when *su compinodori* lies on his back as his horse gallops along the course. Then it's time for a free-for-all, with daredevil feats of skill performed by acrobatic riders.

S'Ardia

There are more thundering hooves, and the sound of gunshot in your ears, in the S'Ardia. Between 6 and 7 July every year, 100 of the most daring and brave horsemen in the village of Sedilo take part in this wild and frantic race. They don't do it for money or to win prizes but for their devotion to a saint-warrior, ready to fight for the rights of the weakest people, the Roman emperor Constantine. One man is chosen to be Constantine's standard-bearer, who in turn chooses two of the most courageous horsemen and they choose three riders each. Wielding huge sticks, it is their role to stop the other hundred horsemen from passing him. Shouting crowds line the route from the village to the church and hundreds of riflemen shoot blank cartridges loaded with black dust. Still at full gallop the horsemen circle the church six times while the riflemen continue shooting. The race ends in the steep descent towards the narrow Victory Arch of Constantine. Horses bolt, the excitement of the crowd reaches a crescendo of deafening cheers but no one seems to worry. It is all part of the ritual that makes mainland Italy's palio races look like child's play. Sedilo is easily reached by car. It is off the SS131 Abbasanta–Núoro main road, a few kilometres from Abbasanta.

Opposite: A costumed rider gallops past at Oristano's Sa Sartiglia festival
Below: Daring horsemanship is a passion in Oristano province

ISLAND
CULTURE

Caught between Africa and Europe, equidistant between the Italian and North African mainlands, Sardinia has always had a distinctive island character. Like the fantastic granite rock formations sculpted over millions of years, the islanders are survivors and just as hard to wear down.

Measuring 257km (160 miles) long by 109km (68 miles) wide, this is the second-largest island in the Mediterranean after Sicily. Sardinia belongs to Italy and is the same distance from Italy and the coast of Tunisia, lying 200km (124 miles) from any mainland. The writer D H Lawrence described it as being "lost between Europe and Africa and belonging to nowhere".

But it also has glorious offshore islands, each of which has its own special characteristics. In the southwest the Ísola di Sant'Antíoco is Italy's fourth largest island – after Sicily, Sardinia and Elba. Linked by a Roman causeway to the mainland, it was the original site of the Phoenician city Sulci in the 8th century BC. While this island's charms are buried in the necropolises, it is very close to the overtly charming San Pietro just across the water.

Although the Sardinians have no strong tradition as fishermen, the islanders of San Pietro are descended from Genoese coral fishermen brought over in the 18th century. Named after St Peter, who supposedly took shelter during a storm here on his way to Cágliari, the island is renowned for its excellent fish, especially tuna. A version of Genoese is still spoken in this very picturesque little "piece of Liguria".

Bottom: Boats moored at Porto Massimo, La Maddalena

Donkeys and Goats

Other islands take their name from animals, such as Ísola Asinara (Donkey Island). Lying in the northwest opposite the glorious Spiaggia della Pelosa, the island is uninhabited but has a population of some 250 miniature albino donkeys. Now part of a National Park, it's possible to get there by guided boat excursions. You may not get to see the little donkeys, but it's also inhabited by falcons, pigs, mouflons and goats.

The rocky coastline of La Maddalena
Below: The distinctive peak of La Tavolara

Ísola Caprera, on the other hand, is named after goats, and is part of the Maddalena Archipelago (➤ 126) – a cluster of 40 islets and seven main islands off the north coast. Caprera is home not only to goats but also to kestrels, green pines and wild orchids and to Giuseppe Garibaldi, the Che Guevara of Italian unification in the 19th century, whose former home is a museum. From La Maddalena, the main island, there are boat trips to inlets and jaw-droppingly beautiful beaches in the archipelago.

King of the Island

There is even an island with its own king. Beyond Ólbia and the Costa Smeralda the knife edge of the island of Tavolara (➤ 122) rises 564m (1,850 feet) proudly from the sea. Pinky-peach granite rocks, villas, a couple of bars and restaurants are all part of the "Kingdom of Tavolara". Its main inhabitants are peregrine falcons and seabirds. But its "king" still holds court in his restaurant, Da Tonino, and upholds the title conferred upon his ancestors by Carlo Alberto in 1848.

SARDINIA
then and now

Famous for its Nuraghic era, the island's history actually began much earlier, in the neolithic age around 6000BC. Always rich in minerals, the island's black obsidian rock was mined from the molten lava of volcanic eruptions of Monte Arci in the centre of Sardinia, south of what is now Oristano. This fine, glassy type of granite was crafted into tools such as knives and axes and exported to southern France and northern Italy.

The neolithic age also had a religious cult devoted to the fertility goddess and her male counterpart, usually in the form of a bull. Burial chambers called *domus de janas* (fairy houses) were decorated with magic emblems and images of buxom goddesses, and standing stones were erected. By 2500BC Sardinia had more dolmens and menhirs than anywhere else in the Mediterranean.

The stone towers – *nuraghi* – that became Sardinia's landmarks were started around 1800BC. About 7,000 of them remain, in varying states of preservation, but originally there were around 30,000, up to 18m (60 feet) high. Just as staggering were the proportions of the *tombe dei giganti* (giants' tombs) of this era with monoliths towering over burial chambers stretching up to 30m (98 feet) in length, capable of housing 100 graves. The bronze carvings found in these corridor-like burial chambers were of the highest standard of crafts-

Right: Romanesque Basilica della Santíssima Trinità di Saccargia, near Sássari Below: The ramparts of Castelsardo

manship in the Bronze Age Mediterranean.

Invasion and Slavery

The first invasion began in 1000BC with the arrival of the Phoenicians, who coveted Monte Arci's obsidian and exploited the mining riches of silver, copper and lead in the southwestern Iglesiente region. By the 6th century BC they had founded trading posts at Nora, Thárros, Cágliari, Sant'Antíoco (then Sulcis) and Ólbia. They, too, were skilful craftsmen and left behind bronze figures, jewellery and other artefacts. Under the Carthaginians, the trading posts became important towns and the native Sardinians were mainly reduced to slavery.

In 238BC the Romans invaded Sardinia, breaching their peace treaty with Carthage, whereupon local mercenaries sided with the Phoenicians and waged mountain guerrilla warfare. The Romans' foray into the interior was met with fierce resistance and they never completely conquered what they called the *barbariae* (barbarians), later to become Barbágia.

A Roman Province

In 226BC Sardinia was granted the status of Roman province and, until the collapse of the Roman empire in the 5th century AD, garrison towns were developed using *nuraghi* as fortifications, roads were built and mining for silver and lead was expanded. Latin also became the main language – and to this day Sardinian is the closest language in the world to Latin.

The next documented invaders were the Vandals, who took Sardinia in AD456, followed by the Byzantines

Torre Longosardo at Santa Teresa di Gallura

who put an end to them in 534. Byzantine domination was threatened two centuries later by Arab raids, forcing coastal settlements to flee to the interior. In 1016 Pisan and Genoan troops were sent in to liberate the island from the Arabs. This was the beginning of the era of Lombard and Pisan-Romanesque style, and during the next 200 years 182 churches were built. But in 1297 Pope Boniface VIII offered the island to the Catalans under Jaime II, King of Aragon and Count of Barcelona.

The Catalans divided the land into 376 fiefs under mostly absentee landlords. By 1483 the number of inhabitants of Sardinia had reduced from 340,000 to only 150,000 as a result of the plague, malaria, failed harvests and famine. Banditry became rife due to impoverished herdsmen. The lawless citizens of Alghero were banished and replaced by Catalans and the town is still known today as Barceloneta. Watchtowers were built along the coast to stave off the constant threat of pirates.

Kings and Bandits
In 1720, after the War of the Spanish Succession, Italy ended in the hands of the Piedmontese, and the new kings of Sardinia ruled from Turin. The problems posed by banditry, vendettas, disease, mass emigration and foreign exploitation continued unchecked. In 1847 there was a campaign by intellectuals and businessmen to tie Sardinia more closely to Piedmont. Giuseppe Garibaldi, the great crusader and warrior, who commanded the "volunteers" and conquered most of the country in the quest for the

unification of Italy, set up home in Caprera and tried to reassure the Sardinians of their common destiny, writing: "Sardinia is the most important and strategically most significant place in the Mediterranean." But the islanders remained suspicious.

World Wars and Malaria
In World War I the heroic valour of the "red devils" of the Sássari Brigade brought national recognition but also a terrible toll of human life as Sardinia lost many more on the front than any other Italian region. World War II saw the destruction of three-quarters of Cágliari in the Allied bombing raids in 1943. Mussolini tried unsuccessfully to put an end to Sardinia's malaria problem, but it took a later four-year initiative between the Italians and Americans to finally rid the island of its scourge. The first year in which no one died of malaria on Sardinia was 1950.

Tourism Today
The fabulously wealthy Aga Khan created the Costa Smeralda in the 1960s, and this became the forerunner of several other holiday resort towns. The invaders still flock in from the coast, and – though nowadays in pursuit of sun, sand and the matchless blue seas – they still bring their attendant problems. There are moves afoot to try to direct visitors to the island's interior, to extend the notoriously short season and to limit further building on the island. Renato Soru, elected President of Sardinia in 2004 at the head of the Centre Left government, seems determined to implement such changes.

Food and drink

"Sardinian cooking is of a poor nature. It is the cooking of the farmers and shepherds who, in the story of Italy, have never been rich people. Sardinian cooking may be poor in some ways but is extremely rich in others, for example it has flavour, intelligence, versatility and an exotic nature."

So writes Raffaele Balzano in *Sardegna a Tavola*, a Sardinian cookery book, helpfully translated into English by the author. He might have also added that Sardinia is organic or free range in virtually everything it produces. And that many of the delicious flavours come from the wild herbs that carpet the rich pasture-land grazed by the sheep, cattle and goats.

Surprisingly, fish was not widely eaten on the island until tourism arrived. Instead meat forms the basis of traditional Sardinian cuisine – *la cucina tipica Sarda*. Lamb, beef, kid goat and wild boar are all favourites, spit-roasted or grilled and smothered with

fragant herbs. A real treat is suckling pig (*porceddu*), which you usually need to order a day ahead in restaurants. That allows time to massage the skin of the piglet in herbs and olive oil before swaddling it in sea salt. It is then slow-roasted over an open fire and basted to golden, crispy perfection.

You will see other offerings on the menu that are not to everyone's taste, even to the most stoic of carnivores. Horse and donkey meat feature alongside offal delicacies such as *sa córdula* (roasted or barbecued sheep's entrails), *sanguinaccio* (black pudding made with pig's blood), or *cordula* (lamb tripe stewed, grilled or fried).

Above: A busy café terrace on the Via Roma, Cágliari
Right: Top, the famous *pane carasau* or "music bread"; below, a colourful seafood dish

Bread and Antipasti

To begin at the beginning, no meal is complete without the highly individualistic bread of Sardinia. *Pane carasau*, wafer-thin and baked twice, is the most famous, also known as "music bread" (as flat as a sheet of music, *carta da musica*). It was introduced by the Arabs in the 9th century, then adopted by shepherds as it could keep for a long time in the pastures. It is delicious served with salt and warm olive oil and sprinkled with herbs. Although antipasti are more Italian than Sardinian, you will find that both *di terra* (salamis and other cold cuts, olives and cheeses) and *di mare* (seafood and fish) feature on many menus.

Pasta Sardinian-style

As part of Italy, pizza and pasta have an enthusiastic following, but always with Sardinian variations. *Fregola* is like pearls of couscous made into a soup or served *con arselle* (with clams). A real speciality is *spaghetti alla bottarga*. This dish is made with mullet or tuna eggs, which are shaped into bars, dried, hardened and then grated over the freshly cooked pasta mixed with olive oil. *Bottarga* is known as "Sardinian caviar" – delicious and expensive.

Seafood

Although by tradition Sardinians are *"pastori, non pescatori"* – shepherds, not fishermen – fish and seafood are now widely available, certainly in all the coastal regions. *Spigole* (sea bass), *orate* (gilthead) or *tonno* (tuna) are delicious grilled or barbecued. Lobster (*aragosta*) is a great favourite, especially around Alghero, as well as *calamari* (squid), *polpi* (octopus) and many other seafoods.

Pecorino and Other Cheeses

Not surprisingly in an island of shepherds with their flocks, cheese-making is an art form and the delicious pecorino cheese made from ewe's milk accounts for more than three-quarters of Italy's *pecorino romano*. This cheese comes in cooked, semi-cooked and raw forms – made respectively with fully heated, warm and cold milk. Apart from the most famous, cooked *pecorino romano*, the semi-cooked *pecorino sardo* is tangy and hard (often made by shepherds themselves), while the *fiore sardo* is uncooked, white and crumbly. There are other cheeses too, such as ricotta and goat's cheese, but you may wish to steer clear of the "delicacy" *Casu Marzu*, notable for being riddled with live insect larvae. For an altogether sweeter experience, try *sebada*, which is like a doughnut oozing with ricotta cheese and thick, creamy mountain honey.

Fine Wines

Sardinian wines are among the finest in the world, but so sought after and produced in relatively small quantities that vintages often run out after a few months and they are therefore not widely exported. Enjoy them while you can in Sardinia. The best reds mainly come from the local Cannonau grape; for whites look out for Vermentino and Vernaccia. Some of the wines are made by the traditional method of leaving the grapes to ferment for up to four weeks, producing a chemical reaction that has been claimed to stave off heart disease. The inhabitants of the Núoro province (famous for its Cannonau wine) have an extremely high

life expectancy. Their number of centenarians is three times the Western average.

As further proof of longevity, desiccated grapes recently found in several Sardinian locations were DNA tested and proved to be the oldest grapes in the world, dating back to 1200BC. The Cannonau wine is made with these grapes so may qualify as the mother of all the European wines. Very good dessert wines include Moscato and Malvasia, a delicious golden wine for which Bosa is especially famous. *Mirto* (pronounced "meer-toe"), is made from the Sardinian myrtle berry, which is redolent of lavender and blueberry and is extremely potent.

Firewater

The island's legendary firewater, distilled from the winemaking leftovers, rather like grappa, is known as *su fil'e ferru* – "rod of iron". Locals say that it's named after the practice of sticking a piece of wire in the soil to mark its hiding place. But, at around 40 per cent proof, it could also have something to do with the drink's head-splitting strength.

Opposite: Mirto is a potent speciality, made from Sardinian myrtle berries
Above: A selection of Sard cheeses on sale in a local market

Rags to riches –

from the Aga Khan to Renato Soru

Until the 1960s Sardinia was undiscovered by tourism. It was only some ten years previously that malaria had finally been eradicated and visitors to the coast were limited mainly to fishermen or those with boats in search of peace, quiet and beauty. It was the beautiful northeastern coastline, known only to a select group of yachtsmen and their entourages, that seduced the Agha Khan Prince Karim IV. The idea of creating a millionaire's paradise for their own slice of dolce vita was highly appealing to him, and so was born the Costa Smeralda.

Billionaires' Playground

It was sympathetically created, with no high-rise buildings, as a pseudo-Mediterranean fishing village, designed to blend into the rugged, romantic coastline. Now it is one of Europe's most feted playgrounds for billionaires. Celebrities who have homes in the area or are regular visitors include Roman Abramovich, Julia Roberts, Leonardo DiCaprio and Madonna. Silvio Berlusconi, Italy's former Prime Minister, owns seven villas, including the 27-bedroom Villa La Certosa outside Porto Rotondo.

La Certosa has waterfalls, several swimming pools, flower and fruit-filled grounds of 40ha (100 acres) including a Greek-style 400-seat amphitheatre where Berlusconi likes to sing for his guests. However, controversy has raged over the construction of the amphitheatre since an investigation into the legality of the work was blocked by the Ministry of the Interior, and a further insult to environmentalists was the discovery that a tunnel had been drilled through a cliff on the shoreline through which visitors step off their boats.

No More Building

Property developers have been queueing up to build new tourist facilities, but in 2006 Renato Soru, Sardinia's homegrown president, announced a law banning construction along a 1,770km (1,100-mile) stretch of coast. He has made the preservation of the island's environment a personal crusade. "Now Sardinia is safe: there is a strip of coast-line covering on average 3km (1.86 mile) from the sea where it is not possible to build anything. The Sardinian territory will no longer be consumed… The island's Wild West period is over," he said. But he didn't stop there.

Taxing the Rich

A law has been passed against non-resident owners of luxury villas, super yachts and private planes, who now have to pay out substantial taxes. One of the prime targets of the law is billion-aire Berlusconi, who has fiercely opposed the legislation saying that it will kill tourism to the island. Also a billionaire – the founder of internet service provider Tiscali – Renato Soru justifies his stance by saying that he has nothing against the rich, but that Sardinia receives nothing from the second homes of non-residents.

Flavio Briatore, the Renault Formula One team chief and owner of the popular Sardinia nightclub The Billionaire, put full-page advertisements in the local media condemning the tax, but other millionaire owners are in favour of it, seeing it as a small price to pay to preserve Sardinia's beauty.

And Renato Soru remains adamant: "There's the English phrase 'going local' – to go to a place to enjoy a local experience. If they come to Sardinia they don't want to experience something they could experience anywhere, but they come for a particular experience, evocative of Sardinia."

A natural
PARADISE

Shepherds lean on their crooks under the shade of juniper trees watching their flocks graze the aromatic *macchia* vegetation. Eagles nest in the wave-sculpted granite cliffs and wild boar take cover in the forests of cork and holm oak. By the golden dunes, carpets of vivid magenta mesembryanthemums open their daisy-like petals to greet the sun, nicknamed "*buon giorno*" flowers.

Everywhere you go you'll hear the tinkling of sheep and goats' bells. Small and hardy, they are the island's most prolific residents. But, as an isolated island, there are many unique species too, such as the mouflon – the long-horned wild sheep that is on the brink of extinction on mainland Italy. Not far from Su Nuraxi, Giara di Gesturi is home to the *cavallini* – miniature wild horses. The island of Asinara is famous for its unique little albino donkeys. And, if you're very lucky, you might spot a *cervo sardo* (Sardinian deer) roaming in the Gennargentu mountains.

Birdlife

Known sometimes as the Island of Winds (l'Ísola del Vento), the offshore breezes carry cargoes of visiting birds. Home to 200 different species – a third of the entire number found in Europe – many birds come for the rich pickings of succulent shrimps in the lagoons. And many like it so much that they have changed their migratory habits, like the colonies of pink flamingos that are now nesting and breeding in the lagoons.

Opposite: Some of Sardinia's flora and fauna: (from top) an Eleonora's falcon near its nest; a female Sardinian deer; cushions of wild flowers at Capo Cáccia Below: Goats in the Gennargentu

Endemic to Sardinia are rare birds such as the golden eagle, peregrine falcon and Eleonora's falcon. On the coast road from Alghero to Bosa you may be lucky enough to spot the endangered griffon vulture. This is Italy's largest colony of these enormous birds.

Dolphins and Coral

The sea teems with marine flora and fauna and rich, red coral around the coast of Alghero. Dolphins are often sighted around the Maddalena islands, and the Gulf of Orosei is reputed to be the last home of the monk seal (*bue marino*), although these endangered creatures are very elusive nowadays.

Fragrant Flora

Throughout the year, but especially in spring and autumn, the island is ablaze with flowers. Roses and thick carpets of brilliantly coloured *buon giorno* flowers are intertwined with exotic orchids, hibiscus, oleander and swathes of bougainvillea. A thick carpet of *macchia mediterranea* (Mediterranean maquis) covers most of the land. This tangled profusion of lavender, rosemary, wild fennel, herbs, and plants such as juniper, myrtle and strawberry tree is richly colourful and highly fragrant.

A stand of flamingos

The collective noun for flamingos is a stand. Males group together, arching their necks and ruffling feathers to impress a single female. Others may join the dance, and the circling and swirling stand can swell to the hundreds.

Sardinia's Best

Best Beaches
• Cala Luna, overlooking the Golfo di Orosei. On one side of the beach there are six small caves, and nearby, reached by boat, there is the Grotta del Bue Marino. Cala Sisine, also on the Gulf, has lovely light gold sand. Both of these beaches are accessible by boat or by fairly rough walking down mule tracks (➤ 89).
• Spiaggia della Pelosa, Stintino, with its blue, blue waters (➤ 110).
• The white beaches around Báia Chia (➤ 57).
• Costa Smeralda: some, like Cala Liscia Ruia and Spiaggia Capriccioli are well known and have easy access. Others, such as Portu Li Coggi (or Spiaggia del Principe), have poor signposting (➤ 125).

Best Off-the-beaten-track
• Arcipélago de La Maddalena has castaway islands and *macchia*-scented vegetation on Ísola Caprera (➤ 127).
• Tiscali and Gorruppu

Gorge are great for trekking (➤ 90, 92).

Best Archaeological Sites
• Nuraghe Su Nuraxi is the place to see *nuraghi* (➤ 50).
• *Domus de janas* (fairy houses) and *tombe dei giganti* (giants' tombs) can be seen around Arzachena (➤ 129).

Best Scenic Drives
• For coastal scenery, Alghero to Bosa (➤ 112) and Cágliari to Villasimíus (➤ 138).
• For wild scenery, the Monti del Gennargentu (➤ 93) and around the Golfo di Orosei (➤ 88).

Best Viewpoints
• Monte Ortobene (➤ 92).
• From Ísola Caprera over the Maddalena Islands towards Corsica (➤ 127).

Best Evening Strolls
• Along the sea walls of Alghero (➤ 106).
• By the Bastione San Remy in Cágliari (➤ 46).
• The Piazzetta at Porto Cervo (➤ 128).

Cala di Volpe, a secluded beach on the Costa Smeralda

Finding Your Feet

First Two Hours

Arriving by Air

You have three options if you are flying to Sardinia. Cágliari, the international airport serving the capital of Sardinia, is the gateway to the southern coastline. The airport is 6km (4 miles) northwest of the city centre. Alghero airport is served by many domestic airlines servicing mainland Italy, mainly to and from Milan and Rome. Ryanair also has frequent flights here. It is in the northwest of the island and is 10km (6 miles) north of Alghero. The spanking new airport at Ólbia is served by international and charter flights as well as flights from Milan, Rome and Verona. Easyjet has regular flights here. Lying just inland from the northeast coast, it is the gateway to the Costa Smeralda. The airport is 5km (3 miles) southeast of the centre.

Cágliari Airport

- Cágliari's airport is called **Élmas** (www.aeroportodicagliari.com).
- **Car rental desks** are on the first floor in the arrivals hall of the airport. Rental cars are parked on the ground floor outside the airport, opposite the airport's exit doors in a covered car park. Look for the Autonoleggio sign and your car rental company's logo.
- Take the SS391 to join the SS131, signposted **Cágliari centre**. If continuing to the southwest, take the SS391 to join the SS130 signposted to Cágliari and Pula.
- The **ARST airport bus** runs frequently (usually every 15, 30 and 50 minutes past the hour) throughout the day until 11:30pm. The journey takes about ten minutes. (The last bus for the airport departs from Piazza Matteotti in central Cágliari at 10:30pm.)
- At the exits on both the ground floor and first floor there are several **taxi** companies. A taxi into Cágliari costs about €15.

Alghero Airport

- Alghero's airport is called **Fertilia** (tel: 079 935039; www.aeroportodialghero.it). There is a tourist information office in the arrivals terminal (tel: 079 935124; open daily 8:30–1, 3:30–10 but often closes earlier).
- **Car rental desks** are inside the arrivals terminal, and rental cars are parked outside in the car park opposite the main exit to the airport.
- For **Alghero centre**, turn right out of the airport and take the SS291 to Fertilia, then follow this coast road into Alghero.
- **FdS buses** coincide their departures with flight arrivals from the Italian mainland, about ten times a day. Tickets are available from the gift and magazine shop, near the tourist office in the arrivals terminal. For travel farther afield there are buses from the airport to the main cities of Sássari, Núoro, Oristano and Cágliari, as well as Stintino, Macomér, Castelsardo and Santa Teresa di Gallura. Note that buses to Stintino and Santa Teresa run only from 1 June to 30 September. The main buses are operated by ARST (tel: 079 263 9206) and FdS (tel: 079 950458).
- You will find **taxis** outside the exit gates of the arrivals terminal. Taxis into the centre of Alghero cost about €20. There is a 24-hour switchboard (tel: 079 975396 or 079 989 2028).

Ólbia Airport

- Olbia's airport is now grandly called Aeroporto Internazionale di Ólbia Costa Smeralda (tel: 0789 563444; www.geasar.com).
- **Car rental desks** lie within easy walking distance of the main arrivals

terminal. Look for the sign "Terminal Autonoleggi".

■ Take the SS125 **directly into Ólbia** (roadworks are a constant hazard in this city, so there are usually diversions). If travelling to the **Costa Smeralda** take the SS125 from the airport to join the SS131.

■ There are regular services by **buses** No 2 and No 10 every 20 minutes (reduced times on Sun), last departure at 8pm, to Olbia's central Piazza Regina Margherita. Tickets are available on board or from the ticket machine in the terminal. In summer bus No 6 departs from the airport to Arzachena, Palau and Santa Teresa di Gallura. Buses also go to Cágliari, Núoro, Sássari and, in summer only, to Cala Gonone.

■ The **taxi rank** is in front of the arrivals terminal. An average fare into Ólbia is €15.

Arriving by Sea

■ There are many car and passenger ferry companies **from mainland Italy** to Sardinia. The shortest crossings are from Fiumicino and Civitavécchia (Rome), Genoa and Livorno. Some run only during the summer months and it is wise to book well in advance.

■ There are **direct routes** from Naples, Palermo, Piombino, Trapani and from Marseille in France and, sometimes, from Toulon.

■ There are many links **from Corsica** to Sardinia, the most regular of which is from Bonifacio to Santa Teresa di Gallura.

■ For **more information** on all Mediterrean ferry companies, visit www.traghettionline.net or www.AFerry.co.uk

Tourist Information Offices

■ **Cágliari**: Information point, Piazza Matteotti 9 (tel: 070 669255; www.comune.cagliari.it). This is near the waterfront just to the west of Via Roma, and helpful English-speaking staff are on hand Mon–Fri 8:30–1:30, 2–8, Sat–Sun 8–8 (times vary according to season). There is another tourist office at the eastern end of Cagliari's Via Roma at Piazza Deffenu 9 (tel: 070 604241; Mon–Sat 9–1:30).

■ **Alghero**: Piazza Porta Terra 9, at the top end of the Giardini Publicci (tel: 079 979054; www.comune.alghero.ss.it; Apr–Oct Mon–Sat 8–8, Sun 9–1; Nov–Mar Mon–Sat 8–2).

■ **Núoro**: Piazza Italia 19 (tel: 0784 30083; www.enteturismo.nuoro.it; open Mon–Sat 9–1, 4–7). There is also a useful independent Punto Informa at Corso Garibaldi 155 (tel: 0784 38777; Mon–Fri 9–1, 3:30–7, sometimes also Sat morning).

■ **Ólbia**: Via Catello Piro 1 (tel: 0789 21453 or 0789 557601; www.olbia.it; mid-Jun to mid-Sep Mon–Sat 8:30–1, 4:30–7:30, Sun 8:30–1; mid-Sep to mid-Jun Mon–Sat 8:30–1).

■ **Oristano**: Piazza Eleonora d'Arborea 19 (tel: 0783 36831; summer Mon–Sat 9–1, 4–7, Sun 9–2; winter Mon–Fri 9–1, 4–7, Sat 9–1). Associazione Turistica Pro Loco Oristano, Via Ciutadella di Menorca 14 (tel: 0783 70621; Mon–Fri 9–noon, 4:30–7:30).

■ **Sássari**: Via Roma 62 (far end of Via Roma, opposite direction from Piazza Italia; tel: 079 231777; www.comune.sassari.it; Mon–Thu 9–1:30, 4–6, Fri 9–1:30).

Admission Charges
The cost of admission for museums and places of interest mentioned in the guide is indicated by the following price categories:
Inexpensive = under €3   **Moderate** = €3–€5   **Expensive** = over €5

Getting Around

The ideal way to get the most out of Sardinia is by car, but it is also possible to see most of the island's highlights by bus or sometimes by train, although trains tend to be slower. Cars can be rented from all three airports (► 32) or from international and local companies in most main cities and larger towns. Driving in Cágliari in particular can be rather stressful, while Sássari, the second city, has a warren of medieval alleys in the old town which are best avoided as they are very narrow indeed. Be aware that many of the seaside resorts are pedestrianised in the evenings in summer.

Driving

- You need a valid **full driver's licence** and, if not a member of the EU, an international driving permit.
- **Contact your insurance company** before departure to ensure you are covered outside your home country.
- If you bring in a **foreign-registered car** you must also carry the vehicle's registration and insurance documents. It is compulsory to carry all your documents while driving in Sardinia as you will be required to present them if stopped by the police.
- To **rent a car** on the island you must be over 21 and have a full valid driver's licence. It is often cheaper to rent a car when you book your holiday as part of a "fly-drive" package. Cars can also be booked through the central telephone numbers or websites of the major rental companies in your country of origin before leaving. If you are travelling independently, several of the airlines have special offers with car hire companies, best booked at the same time as booking your flight.

Driving Essentials

- Drive on the **right** and overtake on the left. Give way to traffic from the right unless otherwise indicated.
- Wearing **seatbelts** is compulsory in front and back seats.
- It is Italian law to use your **headlights** at all times (including daytime).
- If a driver **flashes his headlights**, it means he's coming through, not that he's conceding you right of way.
- There are no motorways (nor tolls) on Sardinia, but on the main highways the **speed limit** is 110kph (68mph), on secondary roads it is 90kph (55mph) and in built-up areas 50kph (30mph).
- The **main road**, which is mostly dual carriageway, is the SS131 Carlo Felice highway that runs the length of the country from Cágliari to Sássari and on to Porto Tórres.
- Other SS (*superstrada*) roads are the SS130 running west from the Carlo Felice to Iglésias, and the new dual carriageway that takes you from Sássari part of the way to Alghero. The SS125 (Orientale Sarda) goes down the eastern side of the island from Palau in the north to Cágliari in the south.
- Many of Sardinia's **secondary roads** are very scenic but also very twisty with plenty of hairpin bends. The *strade bianche* (white roads) are often unpaved and little more than rough tracks, more suitable for off-road vehicles than those with a low axle. Be aware that should you have a puncture or flat tyre, you will have to replace this at your own cost.
- **Petrol** is *benzina*, unleaded petrol is *senza piombo*, diesel is *gasolio*. Fuel stations are spaced at relatively regular intervals along the SS

roads, but most close over lunch and after 7:30pm. However, many are self-service and take credit cards and euro notes (which must be in good condition and not dog-eared).

- **Parking** can be a nightmare in the big centres. Usually parking is restricted to between blue lines and you pay at meters in cities such as Cágliari. Otherwise a parking attendant will issue you a ticket, which generally is not expensive. Average rates are €0.50 per hour. Don't ever park in a *zona di rimozione* (removal zone), as your car will almost certainly be towed away. If planning to park your car in the road overnight, check that there won't be a market in the immediate vicinity the next day, as you may otherwise find your car trapped.

- If your **car breaks down**, switch on the hazard warning lights and place the red warning triangle (supplied with all rental cars) about 50m (54 yards) behind your vehicle and call the emergency breakdown number (tel: 116). If you are involved in an accident put out the red warning triangle and call the police (tel: 112/113) or ambulance (tel: 118). Do not admit liability or make potentially incriminating statements. Ask witnesses to remain on the scene, exchange names, addresses and insurance details with any other drivers involved and make a statement to the police.

Trains

- Trains in Sardinia are rather slow, but they are cheap. **Trenitalia** (tel: 892 021 from a land line or 12 892 021 from a mobile phone; www.trenitalia.it) is partially privatised and runs most of the network. The longest trip is from Ólbia to Cágliari.

- Many tourists like to take the *trenino verde* (little green train), which runs through some of the most beautiful parts of the island. It may be slow, but that is part of its appeal as it allows scenic views otherwise impossible to see from the main road. The train connects Cágliari to Árbatax in the south and Sássari to Palau in the north. Perhaps the most scenic trips are from Macomér to Bosa Marina and between Árbatax and Mándas. The *trenino verde* only runs in summer (tel: 070 579346; toll free 800 460220; www.treninoverde.com).

- Validate your ticket before travelling by punching it in one of the machines on the platform.

Buses

- Sardinia has a **good network** of buses which link not only villages and towns but also beaches (although these, together with archaeological sites, only operate during the summer). The main operator ARST (Azienda Regionale Sarda Trasporti; tel: 800 865 042; www. arst.sardegna.it) has a good service covering routes from the main cities Cágliari, Sássari, Oristano, Ólbia and Núoro. A trip from Cágliari to Sássari takes about 3 hours 30 minutes and costs about €15. For bus routes and timetables visit www.orariautobus.it

Ferries

- There are regular ferries from Palau to the island of Maddalena. There are **two main companies**, Saremar (tel: 0789 754156; www.saremar.it) and Enermar (tel: 0789 708484; www.enermar.it).

- Saremar also operates regular sailings in the **southwest** from Portovesme to Ísola di San Pietro's Carloforte.

- There are also frequent services between Santa Teresa di Gallura and Bonifacio on **Corsica** operated by Saremar and by Moby Lines (tel: 199 303040; www.moby.it).

Accommodation

With the great exception of the Costa Smeralda, accommodation in Sardinia is cheaper than on the mainland. As the season is short in the resorts (often June to September) early booking is recommended. Some good B&Bs are now on offer, and rural accommodation in *agriturismi* is widely available. Outside the main towns and cities many hotels are closed during the winter.

Hotels

- **All hotels are graded** by the state from 1 star to 5 stars (5 being luxury). The criteria for stars are usually based on the number of facilities rather than the standard of facilities.
- **"High season" prices** usually run from July to the beginning of September, and during this time there may be minimum stays imposed upwards of three days and/or mandatory half, sometimes full board. All prices should be displayed prominently on the premises.
- The old *pensione* **classification** that used to refer to a simple hotel doesn't exist any longer, but you may still see 1-star hotels calling them-selves *pensione*. Usually these premises have shared bathrooms. Two-star hotels have private bathrooms and rooms in 3-star hotels usually have TV and telephone. Four- and 5-star properties have correspondingly more facilities and more quality, while luxury 5-stars offer every comfort – reflected in the price. There are several of these in Sardinia, mainly around the Costa Smeralda and nearby resorts and on the coast around Cágliari. All accommodation prices are much lower out of high season.

Other Accommodation

- **B&Bs** have become increasingly popular and represent excellent value for money. Many are in the towns and cities and most have shared bathrooms. For more information contact Bed & Breakfast Sardegna (tel: 0783 216041; www.bebsardegna.it, or Sardegna B&B (tel: 0783 411660; www.sardegnabb.it).
- *Agriturismi* are usually countryside farmhouses or cottages, often with various activities on offer, such as horseback riding, trekking, biking and excursions to sights of interest. Usually they are more expensive than B&Bs but many offer home-cooked dinners with locally grown produce and are often in idyllic rural locations. Contact Agriturismo di Sardegna (tel: 0783 411660; www.agriturismodisardegna.it). Most tourist offices have details of *agriturismi* and, through serendipity, you will stumble across them in the countryside.

Villas and Apartment Rentals

- Several companies offer self-catering in Sardinia, including:
  Interhome: www.interhome.com
  Rent Sardinia: www.rent-sardinia.com
  Just Sardinia: www.justsardinia.co.uk
  Explore Sardinia: www.exploresardinia.it

Prices
The average cost of a double room per night, including taxes:
€ under €90   €€ €90–€155   €€€ €155–€250   €€€€ over €250

Food and Drink

Food and drink is usually of a high standard in Sardinia and, in many places, is extremely good value. Whether you choose authentic Sardinian cuisine or mainland Italian, from *la terra* (land) or *il mare* (sea), there is something to satisfy even the most discerning gourmet.

Eating Places

- Similar to mainland Italy, differences between the **various types of restaurant** are no longer so clearly defined. While a *ristorante* used to be an upmarket and expensive establishment and a *trattoria* was cheap and simple, the two have become increasingly blurred. Pizzerias, too, will often have other dishes such as pasta and salads on offer as well as pizzas alone.
- An ***enoteca*** is a wine bar which has a good selection of wines by the glass, accompanied by salamis, cheeses and a selection of snacks or light meals. You will also find the odd *birreria* where you can get a beer (or glass of wine) with snacks and light meals.
- The ***gelateria*** – or ice-cream parlour – remains perennially popular, as with all Italian destinations committed to glorious gelato.

Eating Hours

- Bars usually open around 7am for **breakfast** (*prima colazione*). A cappuccino and *cornetto* (croissant) is the usual Sard fare, which, incidentally, Sardinians almost never take sitting down. When in Sardinia, stand at the bar and join in.
- Lunch (*pranzo*) is traditionally the main meal of the day. By 1:30 most people are tucking in and it can be a very leisurely affair. After all, everything stops for the siesta and businesses and shops close for up to four hours every afternoon.
- **Dinner** (*cena*) usually begins late, around 9pm (although earlier in rural areas). However, there are plenty of places that cater for visitors who like to dine earlier.

Meals

- **Antipasti**, meaning literally "before the meal", are not traditionally Sardinian. However, you will find featured on many menus both meat (*di terra*) and fish (*di mare*) options – usually served in great profusion.
- *Il primo* is the **first course**, usually pasta or soup (*suppa*), which is a speciality of Sardinia. Usually containing bread and meat, the *suppa* can be too substantial to be a mere starter for smaller appetites.
- *Il secondo*, the **main course**, is meat or fish and seafood accompanied by separately ordered vegetables (*contorni*) or salad (*insalata*).
- **Dolci** (puddings) and **formaggi** (cheeses) are both Sardinian favourites. There are some delicious traditional pastries and biscuits and the cheeses are among Italy's finest.
- Meals can be followed by **coffee** – espresso is the Sard and Italian way (never cappuccino after dinner), infusion tea or something stronger, such as grappa or *mirto*, the local liqueur made from myrtle berries.

Vegetarians

- The fertile Sardinian land produces excellent vegetables but always check that the soups, risottos and pasta dishes are not prepared with meat stock.

- Chicken (*pollo*) and ham (*prosciutto*), let alone fish, are often not considered to be proper meat, so asking if a dish is vegetarian may result in a misleading answer; instead ask what's in it.

Sardinian Specialities

- Baking the traditional **bread**, often known as *pane carasau*, is like a rite of passage in Sardinia. Deliciously light, crispy and thin, it is often referred to as "music bread", for it is supposed to be as flat as a sheet of music, "carta da musica".
- Also unique to the island is **mullet *bottarga*** – delicate, amber-coloured roe known as "Sardinian caviar".
- The lush, herb-scented pastureland is perfect for grazing animals, and produces tangy ***pecorino sardo* cheese**, a particular delicacy.

Drinks

- Sardinian **wines** are available almost everywhere and are generally good and inexpensive, especially if you opt for a carafe rather than a bottle. Sardinia is known for its sweet dessert wines, including Vernaccia, Moscato and Malvasia, as well as the heady red Cannonau, made from an ancient strain of grape.
- As far as **spirits** go, Sardinia's version of grappa, *fil'e ferru*, is a fiery 40 per cent proof; while aromatic *mirto*, made from myrtle berries, is a more potent 60 per cent.
- **Beer** (*birra*) means lager in Italy. It's usually served in two sizes: *píccola* (small, 33cl) or *grande* (large, 66cl). If you ask for *birra nazionale* you'll get Italian Peroni or Sardinian Ichnussa, cheaper than imported brands.

Cafés and Bars

- It's always cheaper to **stand at the bar** than sit at a table. You pay at the separate cash desk (*cassa*) for your order and then take your receipt to the bar and repeat your order.
- Choosing to **sit at a table** means that the waiter will quickly take your order. What you shouldn't do is pay at the bar and then sit down with your drink. However, once you have elected to have waiter service you can sit for as long as you like – within reason.

Paying and Tipping

- At the end of the meal ask for the **bill** (*il conto*).
- Almost everywhere you pay a **cover charge** (*pane e coperto*), which is usually around €2 per person. Service will also be added in many restaurants, in which case you don't need to tip. If service is not included then 10 per cent would be an acceptable tip.
- By law, the restaurateur is obliged to give you an **itemised receipt** (*una ricevuta*), which can be quite useful if the bill is illegible.

Dress Code

- Sardinians and Italians in general tend to make more of an effort than foreign visitors at dressing up to eat out. While most coastal areas are very relaxed, chic restaurants in cities such as Cágliari and Sássari appreciate a little care taken of appearances.

Prices
The cost of a three-course meal for one, excluding drinks and service:
€ under €26   €€ €26–€55   €€€ over €55

Shopping

You will find crafts, ceramics, coral jewellery, embroidered goods and tasty Sard morsels across the island. In cities such as Cágliari and Sássari you will also find good shops and a couple of department stores with some very glamorous offerings and great accessories, especially shoes.

Craftware

There is a very rich tradition of craftware on the island, but before heading off to the souvenir shops try to check out the authentic article (and compare prices) in the ISOLA outlets. The Istituto Sardo Organizzazione Lavoro Artigiano (thankfully ISOLA for short) has outlets in places such as Cágliari, Núoro, Porto Cervo, Oristano, Alghero and, especially, Sássari, which has a big shop in the Giardini Púbblici. Here you will find a good range of handicrafts, each piece of which is authenticated.

Crafts

- **Ceramics** make good souvenirs. They tend to be crafted in simple patterns and colours and some of the best are from the north of the island around the Costa Smeralda, Alghero and Santa Teresa di Gallura.
- Also in the north, Castelsardo has a long tradition of **basketware** made from willow, rush, palm leaves and asphodel.
- Inland, the area around Témpio Pausánia specialises in splendid **wool carpets** in geometric designs.
- Oliena has beautiful embroidered **silk shawls**.
- Bosa is famous for its **lace** – and for its golden Malvasia wine.
- **Jewellery** – especially with the intricate filigree work – is a good buy throughout the island and, in Alghero especially, you will find it intertwined with the high-quality coral for which the town is so famous.
- **Knives** are also a speciality. A classic example is the shepherd's pocket knife, hand-crafted and a real work of art. The finest and most traditional are produced in Árbus and Pattada.

Food and Drink

For gourmet delights, Cannonau wine (increasingly believed to be the elixir of longevity) or sweet Malvasia dessert wine, olive oil, pecorino cheese, mountain honey, torrone nougat and Nuorese sweetmeats should all be high on the shopping list.

Entertainment

The island offers a plethora of entertainment from summer open-air festivals and concerts to opera, cutting-edge theatre and dance and pageants and festivities celebrating a prized local delicacy or saint's day. Nightlife throbs around the resorts and in the university towns such as Sássari and Cágliari – and the glitterati and A-list celebrities can often be spotted in the Costa Smeralda in high summer, when it becomes the HQ of the paparazzi.

Information

- The tourist offices in individual towns have comprehensive listings on local events. For major cultural festivals, tourist offices in Cágliari,

Alghero and Sássari generally have all the details. Also consult visitor centres for up-to-date details of local nightlife as new clubs and bars come and go quite quickly.

Festivals

There are festivals for every season. Some celebrate the harvest, many are religious, others involve shows of equestrian expertise, yet others are pagan in origin. But all are spectacular and a wonderful opportunity for dancing, feasting and immersing yourself in the infectious Sardinian love of life. The following are just a taster:

- *Carnevale* (Carnival, Feb/Mar) is celebrated throughout the island but Sa Sartiglia in Oristano is an extraordinary medieval joust of horsemen in glorious, traditional costumes. In Mamoiada the *mamuthones* procession is of men wearing sinister wooden masks and heavy sheep-skin cloaks parading slowly through town tolling mournful cowbells. However, it's all symbolic of good times and good harvests (➤ 93).
- *Sa Die de Sa Sardigna* (Sardinian Day, 28 Apr) commemorates the Vesper Insurrection (*Vespri Sardi*) of 1794 that led to the expulsion of the Piedmontese from Sardinia. The leaders' arrest is re-enacted in costume in the San Remy bastion, Cágliari, and musical shows go on late into the evening.
- *Sant'Efisio* (1–4 May) is one of the island's most colourful festivals; it takes place in Cágliari in honour of Sardinia's patron saint (➤ 62).
- *Cavalcata Sarda*, Sássari (penultimate Sun in May) is a costumed pageant celebrating a victory over the Saracens in AD1000, followed by a spirited horseback gallop through the streets.
- *S'Ardia*, Sedilo (6–8 Jul) is a spectacular but dangerous horse race between Oristano and Núoro, accompanied by gunshots and thousands of spectators.
- *I Candelieri*, Sássari (14 Aug) sees giant timber "candles" paraded through the streets in the city's big feast.
- *Sagra del Redentore*, Monte Ortobene (29 Aug) is celebrated with a torch-lit procession and fabulous traditional costumes.
- *Festa di San Salvatore* (first Sun in Sep) involves the Barefoot Race, 8km (5 miles) to San Salvatore from Cábras and back again.

Sports

- **Swimming** is good all around the coast.
- **Windsurfing or kite-surfing** are popular everywhere, although the winds are especially good on the north coast. The west coast has some terrific surf at the beaches around Buggerru.
- **Sailing** is the royal pastime – especially on the Costa Smeralda – where it is possible to rent a yacht if you haven't brought one with you.
- Snorkellers and divers will find an underwater paradise in the limpid waters, and there are many schools and PADI-registered **diving** outfits scattered around the island, especially around the Golfo di Orosei.
- For **golf** enthusiasts Sardinia has two of Europe's most beautiful 18-hole courses – the Pevero Golf Club at the Costa Smeralda's Cala di Volpe and the Is Molas Golf Hotel at Santa Margherita di Pula.
- There is wonderful mountain terrain to be explored and **hiked** over, especially in the Gennargentu and Sopramonte mountain ranges.
- **Bolted climbing** is very popular around Cala Gonone.
- **Horse trekking** is very popular in the Barbágia region, and plenty of seaside resorts offer the opportunity to canter along the sands on the sparkling seashore.

Cágliari and the South

Getting Your Bearings

Sardinia's capital Cágliari is a proud, salty port – the island's largest city by far – and a tantalising pot pourri of ancient and modern. This southern part of the island was especially attractive to the Phoenicians, Carthaginians and, of course, Romans, and the area is peppered with souvenirs of their stay. But the Nuraghic civilisation was here too, leaving behind their most complete settlement at Su Nuraxi. And then there are the beaches – some of the island's most beautiful – and all within striking distance of the city.

Golfo di Oristano
Punta Funtánas
197
Nuraghe Su Nuraxi 3
126
Villamar
Mándas
Lago d Mulárgia
126
E25 131
197
547
Sanluri
Senorbi
Gúspini
197
San Gavino Montreale
293
547
387
Arburese
196
Villacidro
Sant' Andrea Frius
Capo Pécora
Parco geominerario storico ed ambientale della Sardegna
1236
Punta Perda de sa Mesa
Nuráminis
Buggerru
Fluminese
196
Villasor
128
Costa Verde 4
Iglésias
466
E25 131
387
Golfo di Gonnesa
126
130
Siliqua
293
Sestu Sínna
Assémini
131d
554
Quartu
Castello di San Michele 6 I
Sant' Elena
Gonnesa
Portoscuso
Parco geominerario storico ed ambientale della Sardegna
Zona Úmida Stagno Santa Gilla
Ísola di San Pietro 4
Carloforte
Carbónia
293
Acquacadda
Cágliari 8 **Poetto**
Capo Sant' Elia
Calasetta
126d
1105 Monte Tiricco
Capoterra
Golfo di Cágliari
S Antíoco
Ísola di Sant' Antíoco
Golfo di Pálmas
195
Giba
Riserva Naturale Foresta di Monte Arcosu
195
Capo Sperone
195
Nora 4
Page 41: Castello is a maze of narrow streets
Below: Tour boat at Villasimíus
Costa del Sud 10
Chia
Capo Teulada
Capo Spartivento

Known as "Casteddu" (the castle) in the Sardinian language, Cágliari perches on top of a hill overlooking its beautiful gulf, the Bay of Angels. Most of the white limestone city walls are intact and the impressive effect of the warm Mediterranean sunlight reflecting on the dazzling city moved D H Lawrence to compare the city to a "white Jerusalem" in his book *Sea and Sardinia*. The Castello quarter is the old town and also home to the island's best archaeological museum, the fascinating Museo Archeológico Nazionale. The lower town, or Marina quarter, is the perfect place for strolling and dining in the maze of little streets behind the Via Roma. The city outskirts may be sprawling and industrial but even there flamingos preen and birdlife flocks in to the lagoons, not so far from the airport itself.

Inland the huge prehistoric site of Nuraghe Su Nuraxi looms up from the hill country of La Marmilla. To the west is the wildly beautiful Costa Verde, while the Costa del Sud has mile upon mile of white sand and dunes on the approach to Nora and its evocative ruins.

The imposing bulwark of the Torre dell'Elefante

Cágliari and the South in Four Days

Day One

Morning

Travel to – or wake up in – Cágliari. Visit the tourist office, then walk around ■ Il Castello quarter (➤ 46). Enjoy a coffee at the Caffé Arsenale, Piazza Arsenale, just by the entrance to the museum, and then visit the Museo Archeológico Nazionale.

Lunch

Have a picnic by Bastione San Remy or try for a table outside in the De Candia bar/restaurant, Via Marco de Candia 1–3, just by the Bastione. Good snacks are available (and at night there's live music from 11pm).

Afternoon

Head for the beach at ■ Poetto (➤ 55) and admire the boats at Marina Píccola on the western end.

Late afternoon and evening

Stroll around Cágliari and indulge in some retail therapy. Via Manno is good for fashion shops, while the department store Rinascente is on Via Roma. Have dinner at Dal Corsaro (Marina quarter, ➤ 60) or at Teatro Lirico's S'Apposentu (booking advised, ➤ 60).

Day Two

Morning

Take the SS131 (Carlo Felice Highway) north in the direction of Sanluri and then the SS197 northeast signposted Barúmini. Su Nuraxi is just outside it. Have a coffee in the bar across the road, then join a guided tour of **3** Su Nuraxi (below opposite; ➤ 50).

Lunch

Try Barúmini's Sa Lolla Albergo Ristorante (➤ 61).

Afternoon

Drive south on the SS197 towards Sanluri. Continue past San Gavino to Gúspini and take the scenic SS126 past Árbus and on to the Costa Verde. Stop for a drink at Buggerru (off the SP83) and admire the dramatic seascape. Continue down to Sant'Antíoco and, if time, take the ferry across to Ísola di San Pietro (below; ➤ 52).

Day Three

Morning

Take the SS195 running along the **10** Costa del Sud (➤ 57) to Chia and relax on the beach.

Lunch

Try a pizza or pasta al fresco at Le Dune (➤ 61).

Afternoon

Visit the archaeological site of **4** Nora (➤ 52). Stay overnight at Chia.

Day Four

Morning

Take the scenic coastal road to **2** Villasimíus (➤ 48) or the direct road SS125 east of Cágliari to the Monte dei Sette Fratelli.

Lunch

Have a picnic or lunch at Le Vecchie Carceri, Castiádas.

Afternoon

Relax in Villasimíus and/or take a boat trip to **9** Ísola dei Cávoli and Ísola Serpentara (➤ 56).

Evening

Start the evening with an *aperitivo* at the Plaza Café on Piazza Incani in the heart of town. Stay overnight at Villasimíus.

❶ Cágliari's Castello Quarter

Known as the *città d'acqua e di luce* – city of water and light – the Sardinian capital is a vibrant place. The first inhabitants settled here at the end of the third millennium BC and its monuments trace the island's history from its ancient origins to the present day. The Phoenicians called it Kàralis, meaning "rocky place", and when you look out from the dramatic ramparts over the limestone hills, this name seems very apt.

The historical centre within the bastioned walls is known as the Castello, or "Casteddu", as the locals refer to the whole city. It is compact and, although steep, is relatively easy to walk around. Defences were erected here by the Pisans after they took over the Byzantine city in 1217, though the present walls are Catalan and Piedmontese extensions. West of the Bastione San Remy, next to the university, the white 14th-century Pisan **Torre dell'Elefante** is one of the only two remaining towers. Look for the sculpted elephant at the base, and the portcullis, which was once festooned with the heads of executed prisoners. A climb to the top rewards with altogether more savoury views from the terrace.

In the centre of Castello is the **Cattedrale di Santa Maria**. It was originally built in the 13th century, but few vestiges of its former Gothic glory remain after rebuilding in the 17th century and a more recent makeover for the 2000 Jubilee. D H Lawrence commented that it had gone through "the mincing machine of the ages, and oozed out baroque and sausagey". However, there are still some treasures inside, including the two stone pulpits (originally one) on each side of the main doors, which were carved for Pisa cathedral in 1162 and presented by the Pisans to Cágliari in 1312.

View of the historical centre and the ramparts

The cathedral's neoclassical façade with its mosaics of a pouting Madonna and child does not appeal to everyone

Museo Archeológico Nazionale

Here you'll find the island's most important collection of arte-facts from prehistoric to Roman times. Spanning three floors in chronological order, the museum's first level is devoted to the pre-Nuraghic millennia, including obsidian tools and little round fertility stone goddesses – part of the Great Mother Goddess cult often found in "fairy houses" – bronze statuettes used as votive offerings, and displays of jewellery, from neck-laces of fox teeth (*canini di volpe*) to an exquisite filigree gold necklace and earrings dating from the 4th century BC.

Largo Carlo Felice

This is Cágliari's most important street, where, in late spring and autumn, jacaranda trees put on a breathtaking display. At the southern end is Via Roma, lined with cafés, bars and elegant shops, and the place to watch the evening *passeggiata*.

TAKING A BREAK

Have a drink or snack at the **Caffè degli Spiriti** on the terrace at Bastione San Remy and admire the lovely views.

➕ 170 B4

Torre dell'Elefante
✉ Via Università 🕐 May–Oct Tue–Sun 9–1, 3:30–7:30; Nov–Apr 9–4:30

Cattedrale di Santa Maria
✉ Piazza Palazzo ☎ 070 663837 🕐 Mon–Sat 8–12:30, 4–7, Sun 8–1, 4–8

Museo Archeológico Nazionale
✉ Piazza dell' Arsenale ☎ 070 684000 🕐 Apr–Oct Tue–Sun 9–8; Nov–Mar 9–noon, 2–8 💲 Moderate

CÁGLIARI'S CASTELLO QUARTER: INSIDE INFO

Top tip Of the two towers, the **Torre dell'Elefante** is the better choice to climb, rather than the Torre San Pancrazio, as it has access to the top terrace.

2 Villasimíus and the Sárrabus

Lying in the far southeastern corner of the island, framed by *macchia* and pines, the former fishing village of Villasimíus is now a popular resort almost unfairly endowed with beautiful beaches nearby. To the north is the Sárrabus, a wild region dominated by the Sette Fratelli mountains – a natural oasis covered in rich forestland.

Cycling through Villasimíus

The busiest part of Villasimíus is along the main street, Via Umberto I, which widens out at the two main squares, Piazza Gramsci and Piazza Incani, at the heart of town. The **tourist information centre** is usually located at Piazza Gramsci – a good place to pick up information on boat trips around the area, especially to the islands of Cávoli and Serpentara.

Off Via Umberto I on Via Frau is the **Museo Archeológico**, showcasing local finds from Phoenician and Roman settlements and a "room of the Spanish wreckage", devoted to artefacts recovered from a 16th-century shipwreck.

Spiaggia Simius is the nearest beach, 1.5km (1 mile) down Via del Mare. It has fine, white sand lapped by azure-green shallow seas. From here there are magnificent views of the offshore islands of **Cávoli and Serpentara**. Towards the south, the beach joins the Spiaggia Porto Giunco-Notteri. This is another enchanting corner of Villasimíus, separating the sea from the lagoon of Notteri, which is frequently home to a host of pink flamingos. On the western side the sands of

Spiaggia del Riso is reminiscent of white grains of rice, hence the name "del Riso" (of rice). In fact they're minuscule grains of translucent quartz.

The headland of **Capo Carbonara**, complete with old fortress and harbour, is the most southeasterly point of Sardinia. From here the high coast road north to Costa Rei is extraordinarily scenic. Many glorious beaches lie all the way along here.

The Sárrabus

This wild corner of Sardinia is known as the Sárrabus. At its heart are the rugged peaks of the **Monte dei Sette Fratelli** (Seven Brothers) rising to 1,023m (3,356 feet). They are inhabited by some of the island's last remaining deer, who take cover under the mantle of fragrant *macchia*, cork and holm oak. The area is also rich in wild boar, hare and birdlife.

The winding and very scenic SS125 east of Cágliari goes north to the Monte dei Sette Fratelli. About 29km (18 miles) out of Cágliari you come to a left fork for Burcei. Opposite this turn-off is the Caserma Forestale. Here you can obtain maps of all the walks in the area, ranging from short mile-long loops to all-day treks. To the northwest of Villasimíus, off the SP17 at **Castiádas**, there is a very good access point for the Monte dei Sette Fratelli, and the Cooperativa Monte dei Sette Fratelli here has a huge array of excursions on offer. The town was a penal colony in the 19th century, and the buildings have now been restored.

The shoreline at Villasimíus is backed by flower-studded meadows

TAKING A BREAK

The **Café del Porto** by the marina in Villasimíus is a good bet.

➕ Villasimíus 169 D1; Sárrabus 168 C3

Museo Archeológico
✉ Via Frau 🕐 Mid-June to mid-Sep Tue–Fri 10–1, 9–midnight; mid-Sep to mid-Jun Tue–Thu 10–1, Fri–Sun 10–1, 5–7

VILLASIMÍUS AND THE SÁRRABUS: INSIDE INFO

Hidden gem The village of Burcei in the Monte dei Sette Fratelli is famous for its cherry blossom, which bursts into flower in May.

3 Nuraghe Su Nuraxi

In Sardinian dialect, *su nuraxi* means simply "the *nuraghi*". This site is the largest and most important Nuraghic complex on the island and is a Unesco World Heritage Site. It looks like a beehive, surrounded by a honeycomb of the remains of buildings.

The complex at Barúmini, which was extended and reinforced in the first half of the first millennium BC under the Carthaginians, is the finest and most complete example of this remarkable form of prehistoric architecture. Visible for miles around, the main central tower of Su Nuraxi towers over a small plain, surrounded by other *nuraghi* to form a star-shaped system. Yet for centuries it was buried among the other hills of the Marmilla area. It wasn't until 1949 that excavation began by the Sardinian archaeologist Giovanni Liulli, who became convinced that the hummock concealed Nuraghic treasures. It took six years to uncover it and excavations still continue today.

Looking down inside the main tower

Guided Tours

Guided tours depart from the ticket office and bookshop on the half hour in the company of a guide who is usually multilingual. You are not allowed to walk on the site unaccompanied as it is potentially quite dangerous. The terrain is very uneven and some scrambling up and down in confined spaces is necessary.

The oldest section is the huge three-storey central tower that was originally some 18m (60 feet) high but is now 13.7m (45 feet). It is estimated to date back to 1500BC and is thought to have been buried by the Sards and Carthaginians during the time of the Roman conquest. What remains today is remarkably well preserved.

Built of dark basalt blocks, the central tower is believed to have been constructed from volcanic stone transported from 10km (6 miles) away. The scale of Nuraghic constructions varied greatly, depending on the function and importance of the buildings. Here, the fortress had a bastion with four towers at the corners.

The bastion towers led to the courtyard through long corridors. The lower chamber at the end of a corridor is of the "tholos" type, where the roof is corbelled or a "false cupola" built by laying successive stones so that each course overhangs the previous one. To get here you have to negotiate narrow, dimly lit passageways and steps hewn from the rock. From the top there are superb views of the whole site and of the more than 200 horseshoe-shaped roofless buildings of the surrounding Nuraghic village, some of which have now been reconstructed.

TAKING A BREAK

Have a coffee or a snack in the **bar** opposite the entrance to Su Nuraxi.

The surviving walls show the shape of the rooms

🔢 168 A5   ✉ Su Nuraxi, Barúmini   ☎ 070 936 8128   🕐 Daily 9–dusk. Entry by guided tour only, running on the half hour   💶 Expensive

NURAGHE SU NURAXI: INSIDE INFO

Top tips You need to have **strong shoes** for negotiating the rough terrain of Su Nuraxi, and the site is not at all suitable for those who find walking difficult.

• In Barúmini the **Casa Zapata** (tel: 070 936 8476) has some finds on display from Su Nuraxi, but the most comprehensive display is at the Museo Archeológico in Cágliari.

Hidden gem Nearby (1km/0.6 mile west of Barúmini) is **Sardegna in Miniatura** (right), a miniature model island of Sardinia complete with scaled-down version of huts in a Nuraghic village and a play area, which is ideal for children (open Easter–Sep daily 9–8; Oct–Easter 9–5).

4 Nora and the Southwest

Also known as the Sulcis, this southwest corner has magnificent beaches, dramatic coastline, unspoilt islands and classic Phoenician and Roman remains. There are vestiges too of the old mine galleries, dating from a time when there was extensive mining for silver, zinc, lead and many other minerals.

Nora was the first city on the island to be founded by the Phoenicians in the 8th century BC. Strategically positioned on the Capo di Pula promontory, it had three harbours, so ensuring that at least one of them would be sheltered from the winds. It was expanded by the Romans to become the most important city in Sardinia, but began to decline in the 5th century AD when rising seas submerged a third of the site.

It is an evocative place, encircled by fragrant umbrella pines and overlooking a pretty beach. Most of the remains date to the Roman period. Highlights include the theatre, which was the only one on the island that staged plays rather than gladiatorial shows (and it still used for open-air concerts in summer), and the **Thermae** (baths) of which there were four, for people of different classes.

Some fine mosaic floors survive at Nora in the remains of a patrician villa and in the Forum

Ísola di San Pietro

The very pretty Ísola di San Pietro is reached by a half-hour ferry ride from the island of Sant'Antíoco. As the first sight of Carloforte, San Pietro's only town, comes into view, you could easily imagine yourself to be in mainland Italy's Liguria. Pastel-coloured houses cluster around the harbour and little alleys, and the main street bears the name Via Genova. None of this is surprising when you discover that a colony of Genoese coral fishermen came here to settle in 1738; a version of old Genoese is still spoken today.

San Pietro is the perfect place for relaxing and taking a boat trip around the dramatic coastline and **Punta delle Colonne** rock formations.

Rock forma-
tions at Punta
delle Colonne

Costa Verde

The southwestern Costa Verde (Green Coast) covers the areas of Gonnesa, Iglésias, Buggerru and Árbus. It is characterised by vast sand dunes – among the largest in Europe – sculpted along the shores, caused by the frequent northwesterly winds.

There is not a great deal to see in Árbus except the **Museo del Coltello Sardo**, which is devoted to the Sardinian knife, with its distinctive round, flat blade. Outside is the largest knife in the world, 3.35m (11 feet) long and named in the *Guinness Book of Records* since 1986.

Just north of Buggerru is one of the island's not-to-be-missed golden beaches – **Spiaggia San Nicolò**, which is never crowded, even in high season.

TAKING A BREAK

Enjoy a fish feast at **Pizzeria San Nicolò**, Buggerru.

Nora
➕ 167 E1 ✉ Zona Archeológica 🕐 Daily 9–7:30 💷 Moderate. Entrance also gives admission to the Museo Archeológico in Pula

Ísola di San Pietro
➕ 166 A3 🚢 Ferries from Sant'Antíoco depart from Calasetta, every hour with Saremar ferries; less frequently with Delcomar 💷 Foot passenger inexpensive, car moderate

Museo del Coltello Sardo
➕ 166 C5 ✉ Via Roma 15, Árbus ☎ 070 975 9220; www.museodelcotello.it 🕐 Mon–Fri 8–noon, 4–8 💷 Free

---

NORA AND THE SOUTHWEST: INSIDE INFO

In more depth San Pietro is famous for its **tuna fish**. The annual *mattanza* (slaughter) takes place from late May to mid-June. There is photographic evidence of this bloody ritual in Carloforte's Museo Cívico.

One to miss Try to give the very polluted area around Sarròch with its smoking chimneys a very wide berth; it's 7km (4 miles) north of Pula.

At Your Leisure

5 Villanova

Villanova, on the eastern side of
Cágliari, is modern and bustling and
has a vibrant artisan quarter. At its
heart, the Via S Giovanni is door-to-
door carpenters, inlayers, restorers,
leather workers, even barbers, all
plying their trade. This area is also
home to some of Cágliari's most
famous churches.

The church of San Domenico was
built in 1254. Severely bombed in
1943, it was largely rebuilt in 1954.
However, there still remain interesting parts of the old structure (dating
from 1400 to 1580). These remains
include the Chapel of the Rosario
(1580) and the elaborate Chiostro
(cloister), three sides of which are
fortunately intact, including the
crypt which contains parts of the
late-Gothic building.

The Basilica di San Saturno on
Piazza San Cosimo is one of
Sardinia's oldest churches. An example of Palaeo-Christian architecture,
it was built in the 5th century in
dedication to the Christian martyr
Saturnius, who was killed on this
spot during Emperor Diocletian's

reign in AD304. It was later converted
as a basilica in 1089. Recent excavation has revealed that it was originally a pre-Christian and Christian
necropolis. The interior is stark and
devoid of any decoration, but you
can see the necropolis, which is still
being excavated, through the glass
walls on either side of the nave.

✚ 170 C5

San Domenico
✉ Piazza San Domenico ☎ 070 662
837 🕐 Admission by appointment only

San Saturno
✉ Piazza San Cosimo (on the corner of
Via Dante) 🕐 Mon–Sat 9–1 💷 Free

6 Castello di San Michele

The Spanish fortress stands proud on
a hill on the northwestern outskirts
of Cágliari. It started as a Byzantine
tower in the 10th century and was
expanded to include a Romanesque
church (11th century), Pisan walls
(13th century) and, under the
Catalans, two more towers (14th
century). Its chequered history
has included a spell as a luxurious

Window balconies in Villanova

The Castello di San Michele

residence belonging to the 15th-century Carroz family, who "acquired" decorative stone and marble pieces from the Basilica di San Saturnino to repair the castle's walls. During the great plague of 1652 it was a victims' hospital, and later a general hospital from 1820 to 1848. It was taken over by the Fascists in the 1930s and is now an exhibition centre. The views from the castle are spectacular – right across the Bay of Cágliari and the Campidano Plain – and best enjoyed at sunset.

🚩 168 B2 ✉ Via Sirai ☎ 070 500 656 🕐 Jun–Sep Mon–Sat 10–1, 5–10, Sun 10–1, 3–6; Oct–May daily 10–1, 3-6 🚌 City bus 5 💶 Moderate

7 Orto Botánico

Under a shady ficus tree opposite a lily pond and fountain the bronze bust of the founder, Patrizio Gennari (1820–97), greets you. This is one of Italy's most famous botanical gardens and has over 500 species of tropical and Mediterranean plants. Among the exotic plants and trees bearing lemons the size of melons are the remains of Roman wells and cisterns and an interesting display of medicinal or "curative" plants. It is a cool retreat for a stroll among some prized specimens.

🚩 170 A5 ✉ Viale Sant' Ignazio da Láconi 🕐 Mon–Sat 8–1:30, 3–6,Sun 8–1:30 💶 Inexpensive. Guided visits in English sometimes available

8 Poetto and Marina Píccola

For sun, sand and relaxation, Poetto Beach is the magnet for the local Cagliaritani and visitors alike. The 6km (4-mile) stretch of soft, white sand lapped by clear, turquoise sea is beautifully framed by the mountains of the Sárrabus and Capo Carbonara. It is also backed by the lagoon of Molentargius, frequented by flamingos and many other species of wetland bird. At the southern end a rocky promontory, known as the Sella del Diávolo (Devil's Saddle), rears above the marina. Legend has it that the Archangel Gabriel won a

Bright beach huts, Poetto

View out to the lighthouse on Ísola dei Cávoli

tussle with the Devil here and threw him off his sella, chasing him away with his band of angels – also giving the name Golfo degli Ángeli (Angels' Bay) to the Gulf of Cágliari. Loungers and parasols are available for hire (€10 each) and there are plenty of watersports available such as wind-surfing, pedalos and canoes. The beach bristles with bars and cafés.

The Quartu Sant'Elena beach is the continuation of Poetto towards the east. At the other end, the west-ernmost point of Poetto, Marina Píccola, is also the liveliest part of the beach. Protected by the Sella del Diávolo promontory, the picturesque yacht basin is a fashionable local meeting place and sailing centre. In high summer there's a concert area

and an open-air cinema.

168 B2 **Bus PF, PQ from Piazza Matteotti**

🄯 Ísola dei Cávoli and Ísola Serpentara

The Capo Carbonara is the south-easternmost point of Sardinia, south of Villasimíus. The Capo Carbonara Protected Marine Area is a sea reserve protecting the coastline from Capo Boi to Punta Is Cappuccinus, including the idyllic little islands of Cávoli and Serpentara. However, it's still possible to take a boat trip to these islands as part of an excursion. The Ísola dei Cávoli is rather unpoet-ically named "cabbage island", bely-ing its castaway feel. A kind of wild *cávoli* (cabbage) plant does grow here in profusion together with Mediterranean *macchia*, wild carrot, garlic, myrtle and sea fennel. From the granite rocks there are magnificent views across to swathes of white beaches as far as the Gulf of Cágliari. The rough, jagged coastline of granite rock is interspersed with tiny beaches, and the sea teems with marine life as it is now a protected marine park. Submerged in the water off the coast of the Ísola dei Cávoli lies a statue of the Madonna of shipwrecked sailors, to whom a feast day is dedicated, the Festa della Madonna del Naufrago. Every year on the second Sunday of July a procession of boats reaches the location and a scuba priest recites a prayer at a depth of 10m (33 feet).

Ísola Serpentara takes its name from its elongated shape as it snakes out along the sea, or possibly from the rare fly-trapping plant that flourishes on the island, the snake flower or *Helicodiceros muscivorus*. Like Cávoli, the island is granite rock covered with *macchia* and there is also a Spanish tower. Like Cávoli, it is a perfect perch for the seagulls.

Cávoli island has been classified a Zone B protected area, which means scuba diving, fishing and unauthorised navigation are normally forbidden. Swimming and navigation with small, low speed craft are permitted but fishing and scuba diving need official permission. The area of sea between Serpentara and Sardinia has been declared a Zone A Marine Park, which means it is totally protected and not even navigation is allowed.

🔶 Ísola dei Cavoli 169 D1, Ísola Serpentara 169 E1,
☎ Boat trips on the sailing schooner *Matilda* 340 067 6054/330 638234
🕐 From the marina/port daily in season (weather permitting) 10:30–4:30, with two stops for swimming 🍴 Expensive, lunch and drinks included

🔟 Costa del Sud

Southwest of Cágliari, the coastal road along the Costa del Sud is one of the island's most

scenic. Punctuated by rugged cliffs, coves and Spanish watchtowers, the snaking coastline is awash with sparkling blue seas and soft, sugar-white sands and dunes.

Rated among the top five in Europe, the beaches at Báia Chia are beautiful, with soft white sand and dunes, partly flanked by lagoons rich in local flora and fauna and backed by juniper trees. Walk up to the Torre di Chia – a 16th-century stone tower that was once part of an imposing network of sea defences to repel Turkish pirates and invaders. The Spiaggia Sa Colonia is one of the most glorious beaches and overlooks the site of the ancient Phoenician-Punic city of Bithia.

Between Chia and Pula, the Spiaggia di Santa Margherita has a long white stretch of sand and a backdrop of scented *macchia* and pines. Capo Cala Cipolla is next to Báia Chia and only accessible by foot, but its picturesque beach and cliffs make it well worth the effort. It also has seven reefs – a paradise for scuba divers. This 20km (12-mile) stretch of coast is accessed by heading west from Cágliari along the SS195 onto the Strada della Costa, which follows the unfurling spectacular coastal panoramas.

🔶 167 D1 ⊠ Porto Turistico di Cala Verde, Santa Margherita di Pula
☎ 070 924 1042 (tourist office)

Diving
⊠ Roberto Spinelli & Stefano Barbareschi c/o Grand Hotel Chia Laguna, Località Chia, Domus de Maria

Where to... Stay

Prices
Expect to pay per double room, per night
€ under €90   €€ €90–€155   €€€ €155–€250   €€€€ over €250

CÁGLIARI

Hotel AeR Bundes Jack Vittoria €

➕ **170 B4** ✉ **Via Roma 75** ☎ **070 657970; fax: 070 667970; email: hotel.aerbundesjack@libero.it**

In the heart of town on the Via Roma with superb sea views, this historic building houses a characterful 2-star hotel on the third floor (with a lift). Established in 1938, the high ceilings, Murano glass, antique tiles, balconies, air-conditioned and spotless rooms and bathrooms give this family-run establishment more than a feel of faded elegance. For the best views, choose the sea-facing rooms with balconies, which carry a supplement. The family also runs the Bed and Breakfast Vittoria next door.

Hotel Calamosca €€

This large beach hotel has an excellent position right on the seafront. It overlooks a cove near the lighthouse on Capo Sant'Elia and is very convenient for Poetto. Most rooms have a balcony overlooking the garden or bay; the sea-facing rooms have a small supplement but are the ones to choose. There is a pleasant garden and direct access to two beaches, one of which is the hotel's private rocky beach at the bottom of the garden, the other public with beach bar. It is about 2km (1 mile) from the centre of the town and the port, and 10km (6 miles) from the airport of Elmas.

➕ **167 F3** ✉ **Viale Calamosca** ☎ **070 371 628; fax: 070 370 346; www.hotelcalamosca.it**

T Hotel €€€

This is Cágliari's first designer hotel. The 15-storey steel and glass round tower opened in October 2005 after the famous Milanese architect Marco Piva had woven his magic, inspired by the colours of the south. There are 207 very stylish rooms themed on four different colours – vibrant orange, fiery red, relaxing green and tranquil blue – and all have spacious, airy bathrooms, glistening mosaic tiles and huge mirrors. The T Bistrot, combining style with minimalist décor and good food, has become a popular meeting point, especially for Sunday brunch. Newly opened is the beauty and wellness centre, complete with an indoor pool.

The hotel is in piazza Giovanni XXIII in the heart of Cágliari, near the Teatro Lirico, and has its own underground parking.

➕ **167 F3** ✉ **Via dei Giudicati** ☎ **070 47400; fax: 070 474016; www.thotel.it**

VILLASIMÍUS

Hotel Cruccuris €€–€€€

Lying in the hills about 3km (1.5 miles) outside Villasímius this hotel, set among flower-filled gardens, opened its doors in 2005. The 45 rooms are arranged on two levels around the attractive freshwater swimming pool and are of a good size, with large en suite showers. There is no restaurant at present (guests are invited to use the sister hotel, Stella Maris's restaurant), although there is a pleasant bar and breakfast area overlooking the pool.

➕ **169 D1** ✉ **Località Cruccuris** ☎ **070 798 9020; fax: 070 798 9018; www.cruccurisresort.com**

Sofitel Thalassa Timi Ama
€€€€

Picturesquely located overlooking the bay of Porto Giunco, surrounded by pine forest and a lovely beach, this large hotel has a wide range of services. The rooms are spacious and all have a balcony or terrace with great views. There is also an impressive Thalassotherapy Spa Centre based on the renowned healing properties of the sea (open also to non-residents) and beauty centre. The hotel has three restaurants and three bars. The name "Timi Ama" translates loosely as "fear to love", as local legend says that the sea and its mermaids bewitch all who stay here.

➕ 169 D1 ✉ Località Notteri
☎ 070 79791; fax: 070 797285;
www.sofitel.com

Stella Maris Hotel €€€

Overlooking Capo Carbonara on the southeastern tip of Sardinia, this hotel has a lovely setting, cradled in the bay of Campulongu.

Attractive gardens lead down to the white sandy beach and there's also a freshwater swimming pool. Rooms are traditionally furnished and the best have sea views (supplement). The hotel is 3km (1.5 miles) from the centre of Villasimius.

➕ 169 D1 ✉ Località Campulongu
☎ 070 797100; fax 070 797367;
www.stella-maris.com

BARÚMINI

Hotel Su Nuraxi €

A stone's throw from Su Nuraxi, this hotel is simply furnished but has lovely views of the Giara plateau as well as the *nuraghe*. It is a good spot for lolling around in the *lolla* – a large Sardinian porch – drinking in the views across waves of golden wheat fields. The restaurant serves traditional fare from land and sea, including *lumache alla diavola* (devilled snails), *troffiette speck funghi e noci* (pasta with raw ham with mushrooms and nuts) and entrecote of beef or horse.

➕ 168 A5 ✉ Viale Su Nuraxi 6, Strada Provinciale Barúmini–Tuili (immediately after the Nuraghic village) ☎ 070 936 8305; www.hotel.sunuraxi.it

ISOLA DI SAN PIETRO

Hotel Riviera €€€

This terracotta-coloured building is a landmark on the harbourfront and is the island's most chic hotel. Under the same management as Le Meridien Chia Laguna (see below), it oozes style and comfort. All 44 rooms are very spacious and individually decorated, complete with luxurious marble bathrooms. There is also an attractive rooftop terrace.

➕ 166 A3 ✉ Corso Battellieri 26
☎ 078 854101; fax: 0781 856052;
www.hotelriviera-carloforte.com

CHIA (DOMUS DE MARIA)

Le Méridien Chia Laguna Resort €€€€

Set in the beautiful bay of Chia, just

700m (765 yards) from the sea, the resort offers elegant accommodation in newly refurbished hotel rooms that have spectacular views to the sea or in family rooms in the Mediterranean garden of Chia Village. The décor is based around soft pastel colours, natural woods and cool tile floors. A regular *trenino* shuttle service goes back and forth to a beautiful unspoilt bay of white sand dunes. There is a popular miniclub for children, a disco and live music at the new Luna under the stars and a Centro Benessere (beauty centre) and gym as well as several restaurants and swimming pools. The service is exemplary and, although the place is large, there is no feeling of being in a resort complex. Accommodation is also offered in the Baía Chia Hotel and luxury villas and apartments scattered throughout the resort.

➕ 167 E1 ✉ Località Chia, Domus de Maria ☎ 070 92391; fax: 070 9230141; www.starwood.com

Where to...
Eat and Drink

Prices
Expect to pay for a three-course meal for one, excluding drinks and service
€ under €26 €€ €26–€55 €€€ over €55

CÁGLIARI

S'Apposentu Teatro Lirico €€–€€€

Slightly out of the centre, across the road from the T Hotel (▶ 58), this new theatre restaurant is already very popular and is the proud owner of one Michelin star. Under the watchful eye of chef Roberto Petza, the cuisine is beautifully presented modern Sardinian with an emphasis on fishy delights. Reserving ahead is essential as covers are limited to ten tables.

🚹 167 F3 🖂 Via Sant'Alenixedda 🕿 070 408 2315 🕔 Tue–Sat

Dal Corsaro €€€

This is a temple to gastronomy in elegant surroundings. The family-owned restaurant is an institution of the Cagliari culinary scene and attracts gourmets as well as those who want to be seen. Service is exemplary and the wine list is long.

🚹 170 C4 🖂 Piazzale Regina Margherita 28 🕿 070 66 4318 🕔 Mon–Sat; closed mid-Aug for 2 weeks

Ristorante Flora €€€

This well-known restaurant specialises in seasonal dishes in a refined, even rarefied atmosphere. Expect all the trappings of a grand

salotto, complete with marble fittings and superb service.

🚹 170 A4 🖂 Via Sassari 47 🕿 070 664735 🕔 Mon–Sat; closed Aug

Ristorante Mariò €€

Red chintz-draped wooden beams and big flowery curtains may not be especially Sardinian, but the Sardinian food specialities are most welcoming. Home-made pasta such as spaghetti alla spada (spaghetti with swordfish) and lasagne with aubergines are excellent. Carnivores are well catered for too, and everyone should try to leave room for the sublime warm chocolate pudding.

🚹 170 B4 🖂 Via Genovesi 16 (easily accessible by the lift from the Bastione), Castello 🕿 0706 53564; www.decandia.esiti.net 🕔 Tue–Sat 1–3, 8:30–11:30, Mon 8:30–11:30

VILLASIMIUS

Ristorante Carbonara €€

This traditional restaurant makes up for its rather lacklustre interior

with large portions and very good fish. Choose your delicacy from the platter of fresh offerings and don't be surprised to see lobster antennae waving at you. There's also a good choice of wines.

🚹 169 D1 🖂 Via Umberto I 60 🕿 070 791270 🕔 Thu–Tue 12:30–2:30, 8–11

I Ginepri €€–€€€

The Sofitel Timi Ama's beachside restaurant serves light meals for lunch and traditional Sardinian-Italian cuisine in the evening, especially delicious fish dishes. The tagliatelle ai frutti del mare in particular stands out. There is a dress code that stipulates no bare torsos.

🚹 169 D1 🖂 Sofitel Thalassa Timi Ama, Località Notteri 🕿 070 79791; www.sofitel.com

Café del Porto €

The only café/bar at the marina and port is a good place for a snack and admiring the views. Spaghetti alle vongole e bottarga and gamberetti al prosecco are typical dishes. There is also a Tiscali WiFi area. Happy hour runs from 6:30 to 8:30pm in the restaurant/bar and piano bar, and the new discobar buzzes from 10:30pm during the season.

🔴 169 D1 ◻ Porto di Villasimius
📞 070 797 8036; www.cafedelporto.it
🕐 Daily 7am–2am

Stella Maris Hotel €€

There are two elegant sea-facing restaurants here, one inside and one outside. The restaurant with verandah outside has an especially beautiful location, with the sound of the water lapping and the rustling of the pine trees in the background. Fish is a speciality here, and there is also a good wine list.

🔴 169 D1 ◻ Località Campulongu
📞 070 797100; fax: 070 797367;
www.stella-maris.com

BARÚMINI

Sa Lolla Albergo Ristorante €€

This restaurant with rooms is in an old, restored country house with magnificent views over the Giara landscape. The pleasant rustic atmosphere is complemented by excellent food, specialising in both seasonal Sardinian and Italian dishes.

🔴 168 A5 ◻ Via Cavour 49 📞 070 936 8419; www.wels.it/salolla/
🕐 Thu–Tue lunch and dinner

ISOLA DI SAN PIETRO

Da Nicolò €€€

This famous restaurant, owned and run by the Pomata family, has a faithful following. Dine on the luscious fish specialities al fresco on the lovely palm-shaded terrace. The selection includes traditional Theabarkina dishes (a local blend of Ligurian, Mediterranean, and North African cuisines) like *cashcà* (couscous), tuna *bottarga* and salt-cured tuna fillet.

🔴 166 A3 ◻ Corso Cavour 32
📞 0781 854048 🕐 Easter–Sep Tue–Sun

Al Tonno di Corsa €€€

Just a few minutes from the seafront in the historic area of the upper town, this restaurant has all kinds of tuna and fish specialities. It also does excellent pasta and Mediterranean dishes, served al fresco on two outdoor terraces or indoors. There is an open kitchen so you can keep an eye on how your dish is progressing.

🔴 166 A3 ◻ Via Marconi 47
📞 0781 855106 🕐 Jul–Aug daily; Sep–Jun Tue–Sun; closed 7 Jan–end Feb

BUGGERRU

Pizzeria San Nicolò €–€€

This is a restaurant with a view if ever there was one. Fabulous sweeping stretches of white sand are often buffeted with big surf (the Sardinia surf trophy is held here in June). The restaurant specialises in freshest fish and seafood.

🔴 166 B4 ◻ Località San Nicolò
📞 0781 54359;
www.ristorantesannicolo.it

POETTO

Spinnaker €€€

The first floor terrace restaurant has glorious views of the Golfo degli Angeli. The speciality is fresh fish and seafood and, like its sister restaurant, Dal Corsaro (▶ 60) it is a highly prized venue on the dining circuit. Downstairs there is a much less pricey but very good pizzeria.

🔴 168 B2 ◻ Località Marina Piccola 📞 070 370295 🕐 May–Sep Tue–Sun

CHIA

Le Dune €

Stop for lunch or a snack in the dunes in this alfresco bar/café, within a stone's throw of the beach. Relax in the colonial-style wicker-work chairs on the sand or seek out the shade of the verandah.

🔴 167 E7 ◻ Le Meridien Chia Laguna 📞 070 9291 🕐 Bar and pizzeria daily 12:30–3, snack bar 3–6

Where to...
Shop

The best all-round shopping of the region is in the capital, Cágliari. Note that shops are usually open 9–1 then close for a lengthy lunch/siesta, and reopen 5–8.

CLOTHES

For clothes and boutiques, from Bastione di San Remy take the **Via Manno** down to Piazza Yenne. **Via Roma** also has some designer shops and the department store **Rinascente** (open continuously Mon–Fri 9–8:30, Sat 9–9, Sun 10–9). The main street, **Carlo Largo Felice**, has some shops and plenty of African traders selling handbags, sunglasses and all kinds of other accessories, some of which are a bit dodgy. Nearby, **Jenna e**

Lua (Corso Vittorio Emanuele 27; tel: 070 682161) is a little shop crammed full of Sardinian delicacies such as cheese, salamis, wines and *dolci sardi*. It is also a good place to pick up ceramics and other decorously packaged souvenirs.

CRAFTS AND ANTIQUES

Near the cathedral in the Castello district, **Via La Marmora** has a plethora of antiques shops and galleries. The Marina district is also full of artisan shops specialising in craftwork and curios. A good starting point is **ISOLA**, the Institute for Sardinian Handicrafts, which has its headquarters in Via Bacaredda. For antiques and bric-a-brac there are morning markets at **Piazza del Carmine** on the first Sunday of the month, at **Piazza Carlo Alberto** on the second and fourth Sundays and a fleamarket at **Bastione di San Remy** every Sunday except during August.

Where to...
Be Entertained

THEATRE AND MUSIC

The most important theatres in Cágliari are the **Teatro Lírico** (Via Sant'Alenixedda, tel: 070 408 2230; www.teatroliricodicagliari.it) for opera, ballet and classical music; the **Teatro Alfieri** (Via della Pineta 29, tel: 070 301378) which stages classical theatre; and the **Exma** complex (Via San Lucifero 71, tel: 070 666399), which stages concerts and recitals. The **Anfiteatro Romano** (tickets from the Teatro Lírico) has open-air music, dance and concerts in summer. In the east of the city the **Fiera Campionaria** (Viale Diaz 221) has open-air rock concerts in the summer. There's a free listings magazine available from the tourist office.

NIGHTLIFE

Late-night bars and cafes in Cágliari include **De Candia** by the Bastione San Remy with live music from 11pm in summer, and the nearby **Caffè degli Spiriti**, which has DJs and live music. Poetto is very lively in high season. The hotels along the coast offer plenty of entertainment, and there are open-air discos.

FESTIVALS

Sardinia's biggest religious festival is the four-day **Festa di Sant'Efisio** at the start of May. The statue of Cágliari's patron saint, Efisio leads a procession to Nora, in commemoration of the saint saving Cágliari from plague.

Oristano
and the West

Getting Your Bearings

Amid forests, fields of wheat, glorious countryside and unpolluted coast, experience the true Sardinia. Of the four Sardinian provinces, this is the smallest – and small is beautiful. Prehistoric settlements, *nuraghi* and the evocative Phoenician/Roman site of Thárros are all part of the west's impressive archaeological heritage. Inland, the horse is king, while the coast is awash with lagoons ringed by pink haloes of pretty flamingos.

Oristano and its province form one of the lesser-known areas on the island but nonetheless a very rewarding one. This "wild west" horse country is the site of one of the island's most thrilling equestrian festivals. The little city has an excellent collection of archaeology and art in its Antiquarium Arborense and puts into context the Thárros site nearby. The Sínis Peninsula is perfect not only for its historical sites but also for its good beaches and wealth of birdlife.

Inland there are many traces of the Nuraghic culture and one of the island's most impressive examples, the Nuraghe Losa. There are citrus trees and silvery olive groves producing the finest of virgin olive oil. Prized as the cattle market of the island, you can feast on the best steak – the *bue rosso* – while around the coast there is a bounty of fishy delights, including the prized *bottarga* – "Sardinian caviar" made from mullet roe. And, away from the flat coast, there is the scenic highland of the extinct volcano Monte Ferru with pretty market towns.

Ísola di Mal di Ventre

Page 63: Tower of Santa Maria Assunta, Oristano
Above: The wide open space of the Sínis Peninsula
Left: The grassy remains at Nuraghe Losa

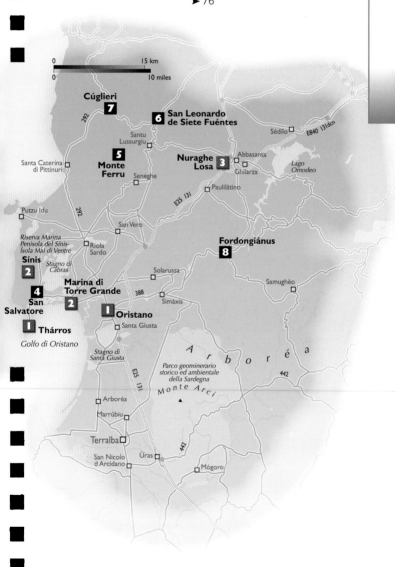

Oristano and the West in Three Days

Day One

Morning
Start in ❶ Oristano by visiting the Antiquarium Arborense (➤ 69), then drive west on the SS131 to ❷ Marina di Torre Grande (➤ 71).

Lunch
Tuck in at Coco Loco Caffe in Marina di Torre Grande.

Afternoon and Evening
Drive through the ❸ Sínis Peninsula (➤ 71), pausing at the Stagno di Cábras (above), then on to ❹ San Salvatore (➤ 75, 6km/4 miles west of Marina di Torre Grande) and have a drink at the Abraxas Chiosco bar. In the afternoon, visit ❶ Thárros (below; ➤ 69) at the end of the peninsula – allow a couple of hours for leisurely strolling and try to time it towards sunset when the colours are at their most vibrant. Return to Oristano and stay overnight at the Duomo Albergo (➤ 77).

Day Two

Morning
From Oristano drive north on the SS131, the Carlo Felice

Highway, for 35km (22 miles) to Abbasanta, where you branch left onto the SP15, signposted Santu Lussúrgiu (15km/9 miles). This is a scenic drive among chestnut and olive groves and craggy hills.

Lunch

Try the Bellavista at Santu Lussúrgiu (Viale Azuni, 70, tel: 0783 552045).

Afternoon

Head north on the minor road signposted Macomér and stop at **6** San Leonardo de Siete Fuéntes (➤ 75). Take the very scenic, winding SP19 going north and west of Santu Lussúrgiu for 17km (11 miles) to Cúglieri. Stay overnight at Santa Caterina di Pittinuri in Hotel La Baja (➤ 78).

Day Three

Morning

Take the SS292 from Cúglieri north to Tresnuraghes and onto Suni. Bear right going east on the SS129 bis to Macomér and then south on the Carlo Felice Highway towards Abbasanta, turning off to the right just before onto the SS131 to Ghilarza.

Afternoon

Visit the **7** Nuraghe Losa, Abbasanta (left; ➤ 73). Take the SS313 minor road to **8** Fordongiánus (➤ 76) and visit the Terme Romane, then head west on the SS388, following the River Tirso for 28km (17 miles), back to Oristano.

Oristano & Thárros

"*Città della ceramica*" is the sign that welcomes you to Oristano. It is also the site of the colourful Sartiglia festival during Carnival. But perhaps most striking is the city's location itself, lying at the northern end of the fertile Campidano plain, surrounded by lagoons and only 5km (3 miles) from the sea. Nearby, the ancient Phoenician-Roman site of Thárros is spectacularly set at the tip of the Sínis Peninsula.

Evidence of human habitation in this area dates right back to the 6th millennium BC before the Nuraghic civilisation began to spread. By the 9th century BC the first Phoenician merchants landed at Thárros, on the coast of Sínis, the ancestor of Oristano. Thárros was later abandoned to escape the increasingly frequent raids by the Moors. As the local expression goes, "*Portant de Tharros sa perda a carros*" ("they're bringing cartloads of stones from Tharros") – to build the new town, originally named Aristanis, meaning "between the ponds".

Oristano reached a new zenith during the Middle Ages when the whole island, with the sole exceptions of Cágliari and Alghero, was under Oristano's control. In the ensuing struggle between Pisans and Catalans, the town sided with the Catalans and centuries of economic neglect followed. However, the town is now reviving its fortunes and is Sardinia's fourth provincial capital.

The **Piazza Roma** is at the heart of town with its medieval tower, Torre di Mariano II, also known as San Cristoforo. The tower is a unique remnant of the city walls, to which it was joined

and which were destroyed at the end of the 19th century.

Archaeological Museum
The top sight is the town's **Antiquarium Arborense**, just southeast of Piazza Roma. This is home to one of the island's top archaeological collections, with displays spanning prehistoric, Nuraghic, Phoenician and Roman treasures. On the ground floor a 4th-century BC lion from Thárros greets you. There are tiny ivory dice, a green jasper scarab dating from the 6th century BC and numerous figurines and ceramics. There are masks, too, recovered from Thárros to keep the evil eye at bay – "apotropaic" masks put in beside the dead in Punic times to cast away evil spirits. Some of the grimacing faces are enough to scare the life out of you. And there are human bones (5th–1st century BC) and terracotta urns with still-born babies' remains from 4th-century Thárros. On the first floor there is a recon-struction of Roman Thárros as it probably appeared in the 4th century AD.

Above: The beach at Thárros Opposite: Oristano's Duomo, Santa Maria Assunta

Duomo
The Duomo (cathedral) is the largest in Sardinia and is devoted to Santa Maria Assunta. Although founded in the 12th century, its current baroque style is the result of its 18th-century reconstruction. However, inside are the remaining Gothic vestiges of the groin-vaulted Rimedio Chapel in the right transept. Look out, too, for the 14th-century *Anunciation* by Nini Pisano and fragments of a medieval marble pulpit depicting Daniel in the Lions' Den. The onion-domed campanile is a symbol of the Oristano skyline.

Thárros
Lying 20km (12 miles) west of Oristano, this is one of the island's top archaeological sites. A Spanish watchtower surveys the scene with two white Corinthian columns stand-ing proud in this very atmospheric, picture-postcard scene. It wasn't until 1956 that excavations began in earnest to reveal this prosperous Phoenician port dating back to 730BC. Although most of what is now visible belongs to the Roman period, there are still remnants of the Phoenician city in a

temple with Doric half-columns and, north of the main site, a "tophet", or children's burial ground.

The Roman city had the usual shops, taverns, baths and amphitheatre. At the northern end you will find a relatively modest 2nd–3rd century AD example of this, partially occupying the area of the tophet. Gladiatorial and wild beast contests were staged here for the delight of up to 8,000 people during the Roman era. Nowadays, there are open-air performances on a makeshift stage by the sea in high season. Sunset at Thárros is a magical experience.

Most of the visible remains at Thárros date from the Roman period

TAKING A BREAK

Enjoy a glass of Oristano's famous Vernaccia dessert wine.

➕ Oristano 162 C3, Thárros 162 B3

Antiquarium Arborense
✉ Piazzetta Corrias ☎ 0783 791262 🕐 Daily 9–2, 3–8 💰 Moderate

Duomo
✉ Piazza Duomo 🕐 Apr–Oct daily 8–1, 4–7; Nov–Mar 7–1, 3–6:30

Thárros
☎ 0783 370019 🕐 Daily 9–6.30; till sunset in high season. Performances usually begin at 9.30pm 💰 Moderate (includes Museo Cívico in Cábras)

ORISTANO AND THÁRROS: INSIDE INFO

Top tips Oristano itself is not worth a long linger, but it is well positioned as a jumping-off point for the local sights. The exception to this is the **Sa Sartiglia** during Carnival (➤ 15), when it is certainly worth the detour.
• The Thárros archaeological site can only be seen properly once you enter the site as the **ruins slope away** onto the seaward side.

Hidden gem Thárros' **Torre di San Giovanni** (9am–sunset) can be climbed for spectacular views – depending on wind conditions. Not for nothing is Thárros known as being on the windy peninsula.

2 Marina di Torre Grande and Sínis Peninsula

Lying 8km (5 miles) west of Oristano on the SP1, Marina di Torre Grande is the town's nearest main beach. From Oristano head towards Cábras, then continue for about 6km (4 miles) until you reach Marina di Torre Grande.

The beach at Putzu Idu on the Sínis Peninsula

Named after the Aragonese watchtower that stands sentinel over it, this is the most majestic of all towers erected by the Spanish, built at the end of the 16th century to protect the Sardinian coasts from pirates. The pine and palm-fronted esplanade faces a wide beach of fine blonde sand, over 1km (0.5 miles) long and especially child-friendly as it shelves gradually into the sea.

Parasols and loungers are for hire on the beach at around €10 each. The beach is also well known on the windsurfing circuit, and you can rent equipment for around €15 an hour. If you prefer to watch others carving creamy wakes across the water, the esplanade is a good spot to linger in one of the many bars and cafés that line the shore. By night the resort really buzzes after the obligatory *passeggiata* along the Lungomare Eleonora d'Arborea. Out of season the whole resort is deserted with the melancholy air of a ghost town.

A little farther south on the Golf of Oristano is the **Spiaggia di San Giovanni di Sínis**. More exposed, this is a good spot for surf, clean, deep sea and fine, white sand.

Sínis Peninsula
This low-lying peninsula west of Oristano is a watery wonderland full of large lagoons, regularly visited by migrating birds and pretty pink flamingos. It is famous, too, for the coracle-

style *fassoni* boats used by the local fishermen to catch the bounty of these waters. While they net the mullet and eel, the peace is broken only by the honking of the ruddy shelduck, indigenous to this lagoon but extinct in mainland Italy.

Looking out over the serene Cábras lagoon

The peninsula's main town, **Cábras**, lies languidly on the eastern side of its eponymous lagoon – Stagno di Cábras – which separates the Sínis from the rest of Sardinia. This huge lagoon covers 2,000ha (5,000 acres) and is one of Europe's most fascinating ecological wetlands. The sleepy fishing town's great claim to fame is as the headquarters of Sardinia's mullet fishing, used in the local delicacy *bottarga* (mullet roe).

For the town's only sight of note, head to the **Museo Cívico**. This small museum showcases finds from Thárros, such as urns containing the bones of animals and children. It also displays discoveries made in the late 1990s at Cuccuru S'Arrius, about 4km (2 miles) away. This was a necropolis carbon-dated to the middle neolithic period (4th millennium BC) – the oldest hypogeum burials discovered on the island.

✚ 162 B3

Museo Cívico Cábras
✉ Via Thárros 121 ☎ 0783 290636 🕐 Jun–Sep Tue–Sun 9–1, 4–8; Oct–May 9–1, 3–7 💶 Inexpensive

---

MARINA DI TORRE GRANDE & SÍNIS PENINSULA: INSIDE INFO

Top tips Marina di Torre doesn't have any hotels, but there are **well-equipped camp sites** (also with bungalows) such as Spinnaker on the seashore (tel: 0783 22074; www.campingspinnaker.com; mid-Apr to mid-Oct).

• Entrance to the **Museo Cívico Cábras** also includes admission to Thárros.

• Cábras can be difficult to **negotiate by car** as there is a labyrinth of narrow lanes around the church, Santa Maria.

• The **Barefoot Race** (Corsa degli Scalzi) takes place on the first Saturday in September from Cábras to San Salvatore and then back again (➤ 75).

• **Birds flock** to these lagoons from all over Africa and Europe. You should be able to see flamingos at many times of the year but they arrive in their thousands in the autumn at the Stagno di Místras, west of Oristano.

③ Nuraghe Losa

Just a couple of miles west of the Carlo Felice highway (SS131), this huge megalithic monument looms into view. It is one of Sardinia's most important and best-preserved monuments of the Nuraghic civilisation.

Encircled by two large walls – the inner one with small towers – it is built of great basalt blocks and is estimated to be more than 3,500 years old. Easily accessible, this symbol of silence lies in splendid isolation on a grassy site, but within sight of the main road.

The *nuraghe* has a truncated cone or beehive shape, built in the distinctive Cyclopean style, which used no mortar – nor indeed any other binding material – but was erected entirely by piling up huge blocks. The central tower, 13m (43 feet) high and 12.5m (41 feet) wide, originally had three floors and, almost certainly, a crenellated top, long since destroyed.

A narrow stone corridor gives access to two of the original three storeys of the topless central tower and several ancillary buildings dotted around the site. The tall conical interior is illuminated by sunken lighting and the walls are peppered with niches and alcoves. Around it there are other later towers, enclosed in an imposing triangular curtain and surrounded and fortified by defensive walls with towers and arrow-slits estimated to date to around the 7th century BC. Winding stone steps lead up to a terrace from where there

Interior view of the *nuraghe*

are splendid views over the high plain and, to the east, as far as Gennargentu on a good visibility day.

As always, the exact origins and functions of these monuments are shrouded in the mists of time. However, as "*losa*" means "tomb" in Sardinian dialect, it may have originally been a mausoleum. Today there is evidence of a prehistoric village around the perimeter wall and, inside the main entrance to the site, cinerary urns from the 1st to 2nd century AD. It is probable that in the post-Nuraghic phase the Phoenicians, Romans and possibly also Byzantines took it over as a fortress. What is known is that the whole "village" was continuously occupied from its middle Bronze Age origins to the 7th century AD. This peaceful yet eerie site is the perfect place to let your imagination roam.

There is a little museum here with a few artefacts, such as pottery and vases which were found within the area, but the major finds are in Cágliari's Archaeological Museum (➤ 47).

Remains of funerary urns

TAKING A BREAK

Have lunch in Ghilarza at **Al Marchi**, near Antonio Gramsci's house, or have a picnic by the nearby Lago Omodeo – Italy's largest artificial lake.

➕ 163 D4
✉ Parco Archeológico Nuraghe Losa, Abbasanta (about 30km/20 miles northeast of Oristano)
☎ 0785 52302;
www.nuraghelosa.net
🕐 Daily 9–5; till 7pm in summer 💰 Moderate. Buy an entry ticket at the little museum/ticket office or at the adjoining café

NURAGHE LOSA: INSIDE INFO

Hidden gem Ghilarza, close to Abbasanta, was the boyhood home of **Antonio Gramsci**, the celebrated Marxist writer, politician and philosopher (1891–1937). His small home in the centre is the Casa Museo di Antonio Gramsci (tel: 0785 54164; summer Fri–Sun 10–1, 4–7; winter 3:30–6:30, but not reliable; admission free).

At Your Leisure

4 San Salvatore

Off the Thárros road and 6km (4 miles) west of Marina di Torre Grande another world awaits. Reminiscent of a "spaghetti western" film set, San Salvatore has a bar, shuttered houses piled together and swirling dust. In the 1960s the Coronca Company transformed part of it into a Mexican village for a less than famous film, *Giarrettiera Colt*, but the place is more famous today for the Barefoot Race (Corsa degli Scalzi).

The festival is centred around the sanctuary of San Salvatore – one of Sardinia's *chiese novenari*, churches open for only nine days a year. The climax is the re-enactment of the rescue of the statue of San Salvatore from the Moors. Hundreds of young men in boxer shorts and white shirts make the 8km (5-mile) dash, barefoot, from Cábras to San Salvatore at dawn on the first Saturday of September, and back again the next day. The idea is that by pounding the ground barefoot the earth will be stirred and fertility restored.

➕ 162 B3

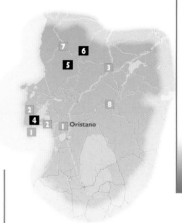

San Salvatore is often quite deserted

5 Monte Ferru Market Towns

North of Oristano the SS292 winds up to the rugged triangle of Monte Ferru (Iron Mountain). There are eight communes that comprise the Communità Montana, all characterised by the surrounding densely forested highland studded with gnarled cork oaks, where mouflon and deer roam. The huge red ox (*bue rosso*) grazes the pastures here, prized for its strength and its meat.

At the junction of Riola Sardo bear right, to Seneghe. This is the heartland of Sardinia's finest olive oil. To pick up some bottles and other specialities of the area visit L'Enogastronomia del Montiferru.

➕ 162 C4

Enogastronomia del Montiferru
✉ Corso Umberto 141/b ☎ 0783
54450 ⏰ Mon–Fri 8:30–1, 3:30–7

6 San Leonardo de Siete Fuéntes

True to its name, there are seven springs in this pretty woodland setting and seven taps from which to imbibe the mineral waters. They have a diuretic effect and some are mildly radioactive, but supposedly have great healing powers.

The Romanesque Chiesa di San Leonardo, hewn out of dark trachyte rock, was built in the 12th century by the Knights of St John of Jerusalem. They once ran a hospital next door, where Guelfo, son of Count Ugolino della Gherardesca, died in 1292 after being wounded by the Pisans. He is buried here.

Just to the south, Santu Lussúrgiu is a medieval village nestling inside Sardinia's largest extinct volcano. Protected by Mediterranean oak forests, it is refreshingly cool in the summer with lovely views.

✚ 162 C5

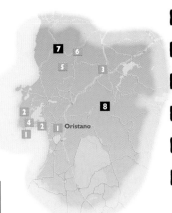

7 Cúglieri and Santa Maria della Neve

From San Leonardo turn back south and go west for Cúglieri. Halfway up the slopes of Monte Ferru, this important agricultural town is, along with Seneghe, the leading producer of excellent olive oil. The silver dome of the 15th-century Santa Maria della Neve is visible from miles around. From the basilica's churchyard there are sublime views of the coast, as far as the cliffs of Porto Conte near Alghero on a clear day. The surrounding area has several *nuraghi*, *domus de janas* and *tombe dei giganti*.

✚ 162 C5

8 Fordongiánus and Thermal Baths

South of Lake Omodeo is the spa town of Fordongiánus. The Romans set up their spa here on the banks of the River Tirso, and it's still possible to visit the first century AD bath complex. The water that gushes up is a scalding 54°C (129°F), and clouds of steam rise from the river. Outside this area is a hot spring still used by locals for washing clothes.

The town is bathed in a russet glow from the local red trachyte stone, a good example of which is the 16th-century Casa Aragonese. Here there are frequent exhibitions of sculpture carved out of the fiery stone, and an annual competition is held in the town in high season.

✚ 163 D3

Bagni Termali
🕐 Summer Mon–Sat 8–10, 2:30–6:30; winter 8–10, 2:30–4:30 💶 Moderate

Terme Romane
☎ 0783 60157 🕐 Summer daily 9–1, 3–7; winter 9–1, 2:30–5 💶 Moderate

Casa Aragonese
🕐 Apr–Sep Tue–Sun 9:30–1, 3–7:30; Oct–Mar 9:30–1, 3–5:30 💶 Moderate

San Leonardo de Siete Fuéntes

Where to... Stay

Prices
Expect to pay per double room, per night
€ under €90   €€ €90–€155   €€€ €155–€250   €€€€ over €250

Duomo Albergo €–€€

As its name suggests, this 17th-century building is in the old centre in front of the Duomo. There are ten spacious, bright rooms, the best of which are set around the charming courtyard. Traditional Sardinian decorations with local embroidery predominate. There is a good restaurant and very pleasant bar.
➕ 162 C3 ✉ Via Vittorio Emanuele 34 ☎ 0783 778061; www.hotelduomo.net

Mistral 2 €–€€

This modern hotel is right in the centre of town. There are 132 functional, yet comfortable rooms, and there are often congresses taking place here. There is a swimming pool and an attractive restaurant.
➕ 162 C3 ✉ Via XX Settembre 34 ☎ 0783 210389; fax: 0783 211000

SINIS PENINSULA

Agriturismo Su Lau €

A warm welcome awaits in this peaceful rural retreat. There are six very pleasant, comfortable rooms set amid fruit orchards. Dinner in the farmhouse, prepared with fresh seasonal produce, is available by prior booking.
➕ 162 B3 ✉ Via Luigino Bellu 24, Riola Sardo ☎ 0783 410897; www.tribu.it/sulau

Hotel Lucrezia €€

A few miles from the coast and northwest of Oristano, this small historic hotel is situated in the heart of the village. The inner garden has the traditional wine cellar, well and bread oven surrounded by centuries-old trees. The seven rooms are pleasingly decorated with traditional Sardinian furnishings coupled with all modern facilities, including internet connection.
➕ 162 C3 ✉ Via Roma 14a, Riola Sardo ☎ 0783 412078; fax: 0783 412303; www.hotellucrezia.it

Sa Pedrera €–€€

Lying about 8km (5 miles) out of Cabras, en route to San Giovanni di Sinis, this stone *casa coloniale campidanese*, or typical Sardinian hacienda-style hotel, is an oasis of cool. Rooms are simply but comfortably furnished and surrounded by attractive gardens. Excellent beaches are nearby.
➕ 162 B3 ✉ SP Cabras–S Giovanni Sinis Km 7.5 ☎ 0783 370040; fax: 0783 370040; www.sapedrera.it

Spinnaker €–€€

Set among pine trees on the seashore, this well-equipped camp site also has comfortable bungalows – some with kitchens. As well as a private beach, there is a swimming pool, pizzeria, laundry, bathrooms and shop.
➕ 162 B3 ✉ Strada Torre Grande Pontile–Oristano ☎ 0783 22074; fax: 0783 22071; email: info@campingspinnaker.com

NURAGHE LOSA

Mandera Edera Farm €€

Once purely an *agriturismo* restaurant, now a hotel, Mandera Edera was established in 2004. Guests sit together at large refectory-style tables for meals with open-plan kitchen. There are five horses to ride and four to breed – Anglo-Arab-Sardo – combining the endurance of the Arab and speed/temperament of the thoroughbred. However, Daniele (leader) has 20 horses for competitions. There are also offroad excursions from the farm. The accommodation comprises four double rooms plus eight suites/huts, which have a hydro-massage shower.

➕ **163 D4** ✉ **Via Dante 20, Abbasanta** ☎ **0785 52710; www.mandraedera.it**

CÚGLIERI

Antica Dimora del Gruccione
€–€€

This lovely 17th-century mansion is Spanish in design and filled with antiques. Gabriella Belloni, the owner, named it after the *gruccione*, a beautiful bird that migrates in the summer to Sardinia from the tropics. Every time Gabriella returned from Rome to Santu Lussúrgiu for the summer season to visit her grandparents' house, the *gruccione* was there to greet her. It is an *albergo diffuso*, consisting of a main mansion and several other buildings in the neighbourhood. All rooms are individually decorated, some with a particular colour theme such as "Camera Rossa" (red) or "Suite Limone" (yellow). There is also a very good restaurant.

➕ **163 D4** ✉ **Via Michele Obinu 31, Santu Lussúrgiu** ☎ **0783 552035; fax: 0783 552036; www.anticadimora.com**

Hotel La Baja €€–€€€

This 4-star hotel is a stone's throw from the Sinis Peninsula at the foot of Monte Ferru and around 20km (12 miles) from Oristano. Nearly all of the 29 rooms have a balcony and sea view and from the swimming pool there are especially good sea views. Sunny colours predominate and the good restaurant has an attractive verandah overlooking the sea.

➕ **162 C5** ✉ **Via Scirocco 20, Santa Caterina di Pittinuri, Cúglieri** ☎ **0785 389149; fax: 0785 389003; www.hotellabaja.it**

Hotel Desogos €

Set in the heart of Cúglieri's old town, this a convenient stopping-off point while exploring the area. The small hotel is comfortable but plainly furnished and rooms are available with or without bathrooms ensuite. The restaurant is very good indeed and attracts a lot of locals. This *ristorante/albergo* ("restaurant with rooms") is family-run and is very good value for money.

➕ **162 C5** ✉ **Vico Cugia 6 (off the main Via Cugia one-way street through the old town), Cúglieri** ☎ **0785 39660**

FORDONGIANUS

Terme Sardegna €€

This modern spa hotel has comfortable air-conditioned rooms with balconies. There are many different treatments on offer for an extra cost, including ayurvedic massage, mudpacks, reflexology and bathing in the mineral waters. The hotel lies on the other side of the river from the Terme Romane.

➕ **163 D3** ✉ **Strada Provinciale 48, n.1** ☎ **0783 60037; www.terme-sardegna.it**

ORISTANO PROVINCE

Funtana Lidone €€

Located on the SP31, northeast of Oristano near Lago Omodeo, this 3-star property is also an ecological tourist centre. Set in the midst of parkland, the traditional farmhouse-style buildings are of local stone with tiled floors. There are 12 good-sized bedrooms furnished in natural fabrics which are eco-friendly but still offer all the usual comforts such as telephone, TV, internet and en suite facilities. The restaurant specialises in traditional Sardinian recipes from the area using local produce.

➕ **163 E4** ✉ **Via Giovanni XXIII, Neoneli** ☎ **0783 192 5310; fax: 0783 192 0110**

Where to...
Eat and Drink

Prices
Expect to pay for a three-course meal for one, excluding drinks and service
€ under €26   €€ €26–€55   €€€ over €55

ORISTANO

Cocco & Dessì €€
Innovative cuisine is on offer here in a variety of dining spaces, including a gazebo, in this colourful, fashionable restaurant that's also a bit quirky. The menu changes to reflect seasonal specialities. Pizzas are available in the evening.
∰ 162 C3 ⊠ Via Tirso 31 ☎ 0783 300720 ⊙ Tue–Sun; closed Sun eve and three weeks in Jan

Craf €€
The vaulted dining room was once a 17th-century granary and is atmospheric and welcoming. The menu is varied, relying on seasonal produce, and has some tasty offerings for both meat- and fish-eaters. Soup, such as *panne frattau*, made of hearty Sardinian bread, is a meal in itself. Horse and donkey also feature.
∰ 162 C3 ⊠ Via de Castro 34 ☎ 078 370 669 ⊙ Mon–Sat

Il Faro €€–€€€
This is a class act, offering traditional Sardinian specialities in an atmospheric, elegant, yet relaxed restaurant. Seasonal dishes predominate and there is a good wine list with emphasis on local and regional offerings. The service is excellent.
∰ 162 C3 ⊠ Via Bellini 25 ☎ 0783 70002 ⊙ Closed Sun and third week of Dec–third week of Jan

SÌNIS PENINSULA

Il Caminetto €€
Very popular with both locals and tourists, the menu here specialises in fish and seafood. Mullet features widely, not just *bottarga*, but also delicacies such as *sa merca* (salted mullet cooked in herbs) or *mrecca* (boiled mullet in pond grass).
∰ 162 B3 ⊠ Via Cesare Battisti 8, Cábras ☎ 0783 391139 ⊙ Tue–Sun

Sa Funtà €€
This restaurant has a marine flavour, with wooden tables and fishing tackle. The specialities, too, are authentically Sardinian. Fishy delights include *burrida* (marinated dogfish), *anguilla con carciofi* (eel with artichokes) and *seppitte alla vernaccia* (cuttlefish in white wine).
∰ 162 B3 ⊠ Via Garibaldi 25, Cábras ☎ 0783 290685 ⊙ Mon–Sat; closed mid-Dec–Feb

Maestrale €€
Set on the seafront with a lovely terrace, this restaurant has a prime location and is deservedly popular. The speciality is fresh fish and seafood and, although prices tend to be on the higher side, this is one of the resort's top eateries.
∰ 162 B3 ⊠ Lungomare Torre Grande, Marina di Torre Grande ☎ 0783 22121 ⊙ Tue–Sun

MONTE FERRU

Il Bue Rosso €€
The Red Ox specialises in the local *bue rosso* beef, prized by gourmets. Other local delicacies feature on the menu such as *casiz olu* (cow's cheese). Reserving ahead is advised, especially at weekends.
∰ 162 C4 ⊠ Piazzale Montiferru 3/4, Seneghe ☎ 0783 54384 ⊙ Tue–Sun

Where to... Shop

In **Oristano** there are morning markets in **Via Mazzini** and **Via Costa** (Mon–Sat) and on the first Saturday of the month there's an antiques and bric-a-brac market in **Piazza Eleonora**. The area is renowned for its white Vernaccia wine, and the **Cantina Sociale della Vernaccia** is at Via Oristano 149, Rimedio (tel: 0783 33155; www.vinovernaccia.com; summer Mon–Fri 8–1, 4–6:30; winter 8–1, 3:30–6). Local winegrowers bring their grapes here to be crushed and you can buy from the source in the cantina shop. **ISOLA**, which showcases traditional handicrafts, is on Piazza Eleonora 18 (tel: 0783 779025).

In **Seneghe** you may like to take a look at the butcher's shop

Macelleria il Bue Rosso at Vicolo Angioy 4 (tel: 078 354171; Tue–Sat; closed Wed pm). Here you will find the prized *bue rosso* steak in every shape and size. The **Enogastronomia del Monteferru** at Corso Umberto 141/b (tel: 078 354450) showcases food and wine products of the region, including the prestigious olive oil and mountain honey.

In **Cabras**, the local speciality is the dried grey mullet roe *bottarga*, known as Sardinian caviar, which is sold by many shops. This is also a good place to stock up on Vernaccia wine.

Santu Lussurgiu is famous for its handicrafts, especially knives, pruning hooks and traditional iron and wood crafts. It is also a town devoted to horsemanship, so many shops stock saddles and other horsey accoutrements.

The citrus fruit oasis of **Milis** produces Sardinia's best oranges for ten months of the year. There is also a wine show at the beginning of November.

Where to... Be Entertained

TOURS AND EXCURSIONS

There are many tours, excursions and horseback riding opportunities in the area. For more details contact the **tourist information centre** at Piazza Eleonora d'Arborea 19 (tel: 0783 36831; www.inforistano.it; Mon–Fri 8–2, 4–7).

NIGHTLIFE

For nightlife, **Oristano** is the best bet, with a good selection of bars that stay open late. Among the best is the stylish **Lola Mundo** café (Piazzetta Corrias 14), which is open until 1am Friday and Saturday and until 9 the other weekdays. On Via Ghilarza there are clubs that are

open in winter only, such as **Ovest** (Via Ghilarza 5), which is open on Friday and Saturday evenings. The **Lux Club** often has Caribbean and Latin sounds and sometimes live bands, while next door at No 9 the **Neo-geo** has more chart and techno music, also with occasional live bands, and is open Fridays and Saturdays only. The **Old Town Pub** (Vico Antonio Garau) is an "Irish" bar with a pleasant small garden. The whole town explodes into life during the **Sa Sartiglia** festival (▶ 15) of costumes and horsemanship.

On the coast at Marina di Torre Grande, bars and clubs line the esplanade in summer, but out of season it becomes rather like a ghost town.

Núoro and the East

Getting Your Bearings

In the heart of the island rise the highest mountains of the Gennargentu. Known today as the Barbágia, this part of Sardinia has never been conquered. This is a land of shepherds, pastoral farming, dramatic scenery and tradition, where villages are few and far between. It also has a wildly beautiful coastline indented with idyllic coves, grottos and caves and glorious beaches of pristine white sand.

Núoro, although not overly endowed with sights, is well worth scratching the surface of to discover some of the island's best museums. It is also a good base for visiting the mural town of Orgosolo and the carnival town Mamoiada. Nearby, too, is Monte Ortobene and the dramatic range of the Gennargentu. Today the image of mountain bandits is still bolstered by some fanciful tourist literature, but, in reality, new roads and communications have tamed those antisocial scenarios, although sheep rustling continues and doubtless vendettas are still waged, but quietly.

To the east lies the spectacular, undeveloped coastline of the Golfo di Orosei. Near Dorgali, the Grotta di Ispinigoli has Europe's tallest stalagmite, and on the coast, the Grotta del Bue Marino is to Sardinia what the Blue Grotto is to Capri. Cala Gonone on the coast is spectacularly set against an amphitheatre of forested mountain and, although now a popular resort, still has a villagey, laid-back atmosphere. From here there are excellent hiking and climbing excursions, including the Gola Su Gorruppu Gorge and Tiscali, the Nuraghic village, concealed in a mountain chasm.

Page 81: Stone sculpture in Piazza Sebastiano, Núoro
Below left: Sheep in the Gennargentu
Below right: The beach at Marina di Orosei

★ Don't Miss

At Your Leisure

San Teodoro

Budoni

Laguna di
Posada

Torpè · Posada

Siniscóla

1019
▲ Punta sa Donna · Lodè

*Parco geominerario
storico ed ambientale
della Sardegna*

Bitti

Monte Albo 1316m

Orune

Irgoli

Galtelli

Punta Nera

Rio Isalle

Núoro 1 4

Orosei

Orotelli

*Parco geominerario
storico ed ambientale
della Sardegna*

Oniferi · Orani

Ottana

**Monte
Ortobene**

Oliena

**Tiscali
Villagio
Nuragico 3**

1463
▲ Monte
Corrasi

**Grotta di
Ispinigoli 5**

Dorgali · Cala Gonone

**Golfo di
Orosei 2**

Mamoiada 8

Gavoi

Orgosolo 9

**Gola Su
Gorruppu 6**

Capo di
Monte Santu

Fonni

*Parco Nazionale
del Golfo di Orosei*

Tonara

**Monti del
Gennargentu 7**

Désulo

1834
▲ Punta
la Mármora

Baunei

Lotzorai

Villagrande

Capo
Bellavista

Meana

*Parco Nazionale
del Golfo di Orosei*

1236
▲ Monte
Orru

Árzana

Ilbono

Lánusei

Tortolí

Láconi

Sarcidano

Fiume Flumendosa

Ísili

Bari

Jerzu

1008
▲ Punta
Coróngiu

Nurri · Orroli

Tertenia

Mándas

Lago Mulárgia

Escalaplano

Perdasdefogu

0 ___ 20 km

0 ___ 10 miles

Núoro and the East in Four Days

Day One

Morning
Travel to – or wake up in – **1** Núoro (► 86). Visit the tourist office and then walk to the old part of town and visit the Museo Deleddiano (right). Walk to the Corso Garibaldi and have a coffee at Bar Majore. Just to the east nearby is the Piazza Santa Maria della Neve, where you can visit the eponymous cathedral.

Lunch
Have lunch at Il Rifugio (► 96).

Afternoon
Walk south to the island's best museum of Sard life – the Museo della Vita e delle Tradizioni Sarde (left) – where you can easily while away a couple of hours. In the late afternoon, as the sun loses its intensity drive (or go by public transport), to **4** Monte Ortobene (► 92) for splendid views across the countryside. Return to Núoro for dinner and the night.

Day Two

Morning
Set off for the **2** Gulf of Orosei (► 88). Arrive at Restaurant Ispinigoli (below entrance to the Grotta) and have a coffee while waiting for tours on the hour. Visit the **5** Grotta di Ispinigoli (► 92).

Lunch
Have lunch at Dorgali's Ristorante Albergo Sant'Elene (► 96).

Afternoon and Evening

Arrive at Cala Gonone. Relax on the beach or take a boat trip to the Grotta del Bue Marino (➤ 88), visiting other beaches en route. Spend the night at Cala Gonone.

Day Three

Morning

Take an excursion (or make your own way) to **5** Tiscali (➤ 90) and/or **6** Gola Su Gorruppu (➤ 92) from Cala Gonone. Lunch is included in the excursions, or pack a picnic.

Evening

Have dinner at Ristorante Al Porto (belonging to Hotel Pop; ➤ 96).

Day Four

Morning

Drive via the **7** Gennargentu (➤ 93) to **9** Orgosolo (➤ 94). Stroll around the "town of murals".

Lunch

Have lunch at Ai Monti del Gennargentu (5km/3 miles outside Orgosolo going south out of town, uphill towards Montes) (➤ 97).

Afternoon

Visit **8** Mamoiada (➤ 93) and take in the Museo delle Maschere Mediterranee before returning to Núoro.

O Núoro

Núoro is at the heartland of Sardinia's traditions and, although not especially aesthetically pleasing, gave birth to distinguished literary sons and daughters whose lives have been indelibly marked by this overgrown mountain village of granite. D H Lawrence followed up his remark that there was nothing to see in Núoro by saying "I am not Baedeker". But then, he wasn't a Nobel Prize winner like writer Grazia Deledda either.

The old part of town in the northeast spreads around Piazza San Giovanni and Corso Garibaldi. On the northern fringes is the **Museo Deleddiano**, the birthplace and home of Grazia Deledda (1871–1936). She was the first Italian woman to win the Nobel Prize for
Literature (1926) and is
one of Italy's most important early 20th-century
"realist" writers. Her
writings describe life on
her native island with
depth and sympathy and
deal with human problems
in general. She lived here
for 29 years and the
museum gives an insight
into life in a Nuorese
house, together with her
memorabilia, including first
editions, press clippings
and her old photos.

**Façade of
Santa Maria
della Neve**

Cathedral
On **Piazza Santa Maria
della Neve** is Núoro's large
neoclassical cathedral.
Completed in 1854, it is
more quantitative than
qualitative. But inside,
among the mainly 20th-
century paintings, the
*Disputa de Gesù Fra i
Dottori (Jesus' Dispute in the
Temple)* is a 17th-century
canvas attributed to the
Neapolitan studio of Luca
Giordano. Behind the
cathedral there are spectacular views out across the
valley to Monte Ortobene.

Museum of Sardinian Life

South of the Duomo is the most famous attraction in Núoro – the **Museo della Vita e delle Tradizioni Sarde** – often referred to simply as the "Museo del Costume". There are 7,000 items here, but it is easy to cherry-pick what interests most in this Sardinian village-like setting. There are glorious costumes, wedding dresses and prenuptial gifts such as the *isprugadente*, where one end was for cleaning ears and the other for the teeth. Gorgeous jewellery ranges from intricate silver filigree to wild boar tusks. Equally fascinating is the display of breads – over 600 varieties – and sweetmeats linked to annual festivities. The highlight are the spooky masks and hairy costumes still used in processions today.

TAKING A BREAK

Have a coffee at the **Bar Majore** (► 96). It is Núoro's oldest and most opulent café.

Formal dress from the early 1900s in the Museum of Sardinian Life

➕ 164 C4

Museo Deleddiano
✉ Via Grazia Deledda 53 ☎ 0784 258088 🕐 Mid-Jun to Sep Tue–Sat 9–8, Sun 9–1; Oct to mid-Jun 9–1, 3–7 💰 Moderate

Duomo Santa Maria della Neve
✉ Piazza Santa Maria della Neve 🕐 Daily 8–1, 4–7

Museo della Vita e delle Tradizioni Sarde
✉ Via A Mereu 56 ☎ 0784 257035 🕐 Mid-Jun to Sep daily 9–8; Oct to mid-Jun 9–1, 3–7 💰 Moderate

NÚORO: INSIDE INFO

In more depth Núoro's other famous writers include poet Sebastiano Satta (1867–1914) and novelist Salvatore Satta (1902–75) – no relation. He chronicled the island's colourful life in *Il Giorno del Giudizio* (The Day of Judgement).

2 Golfo di Orosei

Stretching for 40km (25 miles), the Gulf of Orosei has the longest undeveloped coastline in the Mediterranean. Limestone cliffs and rock formations scatter the coastline punctuated by beautiful coves, secluded grottos and the most glorious hidden beaches.

The Gulf is a symmetrical arch extending from Capo Nero in the north to Capo Monte Santo in the south. It is the seafront of the **Supramonte**, a wild and steep coast where holm oak forests, centuries-old juniper trees and *macchia* extend down to the sea. The royal eagle, Eleonora's falcon and griffon vulture are regular residents and these birds of prey can often be seen peeping out from their eyries on the cliff tops.

Boat on its way to Bue Marino cave

Orosei Town

Much of the architecture in Orosei town is Spanish, reflecting its former rule by the Aragonese. It's a pleasant place to stroll around, starting at the **Piazza del Popolo**, where you'll find the 13th-century **Cattedrale di San Giácomo** with its 18th-century neoclassical façade and gilded interior. On the west side of town the 15th-century **Sant'Antonio Abate** with its Pisan watchtower is worth a look, although it has been extensively restored.

On the coast, Marina di Orosei has a 6km (3.5-mile) stretch of golden sand, framed by pines and lapped by emerald water.

Grotta del Bue Marino

South down the coast, **Cala Gonone** has a gorgeous setting around a harbour framed by soaring mountains. Once a little fishing village, it took off as a tourist resort when the Grotta del Bue Marino opened in the 1950s.

This is the largest and most dramatically beautiful of the many grottos on this coast. The *bue marino* ("sea ox") is

Cala Luna beach has a beautiful setting

the local name for the monk seal, common a century ago but now one of the world's most endangered mammals. This cave was one of its last hiding places in Sardinia, although the last sightings were back in 1992. A tour takes you to where fresh and saltwater mingle in lakes and the light playing on the water reveals fantastical pink and white formations in the stalactites and stalagmites. A relief on the rocky wall at the entrance, showing a dozen dancing figures around a solar disc, has been verified as graffiti from the neolithic period.

Glorious Beaches

Cala Gonone itself has three wonderful beaches, all within walking distance from the harbour. Other beaches such as Cala Fuili, Cala Cartoe and beautiful **Cala Luna**, locations in Madonna's movie *Swept Away*, are all within a few kilometres. Accessible only by boat, the coves are surrounded by crystal waters, perfect for swimming and snorkelling. Boat excursions can be arranged on the harbour, or you can catch a shuttle ferry to the sandy beach of Cala Luna.

TAKING A BREAK
Have lunch at Cala Gonone's **Hotel Pop** (➤ 95).

➕ 165 E3

Grotta del Bue Marino
☎ 078 496243 ◷ Weather permitting, visits Aug 9, 10, 11, noon, 3, 4 and 5; Jul 9, 10, 11, noon and 3; Easter–Jun, Sep, Oct 11 and 3 💰 Expensive

---

GOLFO DI OROSEI: INSIDE INFO

Top tip It is possible to reach **Cala Luna on foot** from the road at Cala Fuili – by a fairly precipitous rough track for around 4km (2.5 miles). The last descent is very stony and a bit of a scramble. You can always return on one of the regular boats back to Cala Gonone port.

3 Tiscali Villagio Nuragico

Renato Soru, President of Sardinia and founder of the Italian internet service provider Tiscali, named his company after a huge silent cave on the top of a mountain in the centre of his native Sardinia, in which ancient islanders used to hide from their enemies. The inaugural advertising slogan was "Tiscali. From a land of silence comes a new way of communication."

In the heart of the Supramonte, Tiscali houses the remains of a village dating back to the final Nuraghic period. Nearby, the Gola Su Gorruppu is one of the deepest and most dramatic canyons in Europe.

Monte Tiscali stands at 515m (1,690 feet) and within it is a wide crater concealing the Nuraghic village – originally a site of over 60 round dwellings, most of them now ruined. It is thought that it was built in late Nuraghic times to escape the Roman domination, for which this was a perfect spot given the rugged terrain and high crater walls. The site continued to be inhabited into medieval times, but was only discovered in the 19th century and is still under excavation. It is a very atmospheric site buried in the mountain with stalactites and trees growing inside and remnants of the *nuraghi* within.

Monte Tiscali provides a dramatic setting for the remains of Tiscali Villagio Nuragico

Trek to Tiscali

It's best to take a guide to do this full-day trek, organised through the tourist information office in Oliena (➤ 91). However, should you wish to undertake it on your own, the best starting point is from the natural spring at Sorgente Su Gologone next to the Hotel Su Gologone, just off the Oliena–Dorgali road. From the spring there is a signpost for the Valle di Lanaittu, a track that is mainly unasphalted so best tackled in a 4x4 vehicle or on foot. After about 6km (4 miles), follow the signpost to the right for Grotta Sa Oche

(Cave of the Voice). Just north of here is Nuraghic site **Sa Sedda 'e Sos Carros** with the remains of 150 *nuraghi* (still under excavation). Walk along the main track past the Grotta Sa Oche keeping left (southwest) to climb up a steep dirt track. Look for the boulder with painted arrow for Tiscali and follow it to the left (east) up a very steep mule trail until you arrive finally at a wide ledge with superb views over the Valle Lanaittu. After another 20–25 minutes on foot, keep left on the steepest, overhanging part of the mountain and take the narrow path to the right over the rocks to the huge *dolina* (cavern) and entrance to Tiscali. In the half-light of the cavern, the deserted village is a spooky but very moving sight.

TAKING A BREAK

Have a drink or lunch on the terrace at the **Sant'Elene ristorante/albergo** (➤ 96).

🚩 165 D3 🕐 May–Sep daily 9–7; Oct–Apr 9–5 💶 Moderate
❓ Excursions depart from Dorgali. Coop Ghivine (Via Montebello 5, Dorgali; tel: 0784 96721; www.ghivine.com) has departures at 9am, returning at about 4:30. Price €40, including entrance to Tiscali

Tourist information

Nuraghic remains at Sa Sedda 'e Sos Carros

🕐 Via Deledda, Oliena 🕐 Jun–Aug Mon–Sat 9–1, 4–7, Sun 9–1

Sa Sedda 'e Sos Carros
🕐 9:30–6:30 💶 Moderate

TISCALI VILLAGIO NURAGICO: INSIDE INFO

Top tips It is vital to wear **sturdy footwear** with a secure grip and ankle support.
• If you don't take a guide, make sure that you **advise someone of your movements** and your estimated return time.
• A **hat and sunscreen plus ample supply of water** (at least one litre per person) are essential.

At Your Leisure

4 Belvedere on Monte Ortobene

East of Núoro, 8km (5 miles) out of town, the road winds up to Monte Ortobene and its glorious vistas over the valley floor and Supramonte massif. A dusty track leads to 49 steps that climb up to an enormous bronze statue of Il Redentore (Christ the Redeemer) at 955m (3,130 feet). The statue shows Christ trampling the devil underfoot and is a site of great pilgrimage. The Sagra del Redentore, Núoro's most important festival, takes place every year in late August, culminating on 29 August, when a long procession is made here from the cathedral.

This is a very popular spot for a picnic in the surrounding woods, and there are a couple of bars and restaurants as well as stalls selling cold drinks and souvenirs.

🚹 164 C4 🚌 No 8 from Piazza Vittorio Emanuele in Núoro

5 Grotta di Ispinigoli

Towering up to 38m (125 feet), the central stalagmite of this cave is the tallest in Europe. From the entrance 280 steps lead 60m (200 feet) down into the fairytale grotto. Nine streams flow through these extraterrestrial

surroundings where the temperature remains at a constant 16–17°C (60–62°F). Estimated to be 180 million years old, but only discovered in 1927, exploration of the grotto has yielded some remarkable finds – including otter fossils dating back to the Ice Age, bronze and silver bracelets and necklaces. All these items were typically found in Punic burial tombs and their function was to chase away evil spirits. Human skeletal remains have also fuelled speculation that this was once a place of human sacrifice. The Abisso delle Vergini (Abyss of the Virgins) is the well that leads into this second cavity, 40m (130 feet) below. Theories abound such as the possibility that richly bejewelled young women were sacrificed by flinging them down the well. Guides will tell you that it's more probable that it was used as an ancient burial ground. But one thing is certain – the subterranean scene is imbued with an eerie, almost sacred, atmosphere.

🚹 165 E4 🖂 Just off the Orosei–Dorgali road ☎ 078 496 2431 🕐 Mar–Nov daily 9–5; Aug 9–6. Tours depart on the hour lasting 45 minutes 💶 Expensive

6 Gola Su Gorruppu

This is one of Europe's most spectacular gorges, carved out of limestone by the river Flumineddu, with cliffs soaring to more than 400m (1,300 feet). The colour of the limestone and microclimate within make this an unforgettable experience. The whole length of the gorge is some 8km (5 miles) but you need proper equipment and a guide to venture a long way inside.

By car from Dorgali, take the bypass to the west (SS125) then follow the signpost for the Sant' Elene Hotel. Past the hotel you will pick up signs for Tiscali and, after

Núoro

The wooded hills of the Gennargentu

about 4km (2.5 miles) of bumpy, unsurfaced road take the left turn signposted Gorruppu and a car park. It is about a two-hour trek to the gorge from here.

➕ 165 D3

Cooperativa Gorropu
✉ Via Sa Preda Lada 2, Urzulei
☎ 0782 649282; www.gorropu.com

🖪 Monti del Gennargentu

Meaning "silver gate", the Gennargentu is the highest massif in Sardinia and in winter is covered in snow. The Parco del Gennargentu and Parco del Golfo di Orosei have wild mountain terrain and coast covering 73,935ha (182,620 acres). There are many villages dotted around; none are especially attractive, but they make good walking bases. Sardinia's highest village is Fonni, lying at 1,000m (3,280 feet) above sea level. The highest peaks are all accessible from here: Bruncu Spina at 1,829m (6,000 feet) and Punta La Marmora at 1,834m (6,016

feet). The strenuous climb to the top of Punta La Marmora is rewarded with fabulous views over the entire island. For a less demanding foray, it's possible to drive most of the way up to Bruncu Spina to the S'Arena *rifugio* (mountain refuge) at 1,500m (4,920 feet), from where it's a relatively easy hike to the top.

The area is thickly vegetated with holm oak woods surrounded by Mediterranean *macchia*. The lower flanks are cloaked in vineyards that produce the famous red wine made from the Cannonau grape, and this area is also especially noted for its *pecorino* cheese. Along the coastal cliffs, olive trees, carob trees and juniper thrive in the particularly warm climate.

➕ 164 B2

🖪 Mamoiada

Lying 14km (9 miles) south of Núoro is the town of Mamoiada. Every year at carnival time this otherwise rather colourless town erupts into a frenzy of shaggy-sheep-skinned men wearing demonic black wooden masks and weighed down by heavy cowbells. These traditional costumed figures, known as *mamuthones*, have pagan origins, and this ritual is an attempt to drive out demons before the spring. They shuffle along, rattling cowbells behind their backs; they represent defeated men and animals and are subjugated by the *issokadores* – men dressed in red and white wielding lassos. This scene is also re-enacted on 17 January for the Festa di Sant'Antonio. By legend Sant'Antonio took hell's fire to give to man, and for this festival bonfires are lit throughout the village. The **Museo delle Maschere Mediterranee** has an interesting exhibition of masks and mannequins (although the best museum is in Núoro, ➤ 87).

➕ 164 C3

Museo delle Maschere Mediterranee
✉ Piazza Europa 15 ☎ 0784 569018; www.museodellemaschere.it
🕐 Tue–Sun 9–1, 3–7 💰 Moderate

Above: *Mamuthone* mask

9 Orgosolo

A painted rock depicting "the greedy landowner of Orgosolo" greets you just outside the entrance to this town of murals. Over 150 of them adorn the streets and corners in a tradition dating back to 1975. Professor Francesco del Casino and his students decided to celebrate the 30th anniversary of Liberation and the Resistance with political and satirical portrayals. Nowadays, many are devoted to modern-day as well as political themes – from folklore figures such as the *mamuthones* to the destruction of New York's Twin Towers on 11 September 2001. There are, too, allusions to the sheep rustling and kidnappings for which this town was once notorious. Popularly known as the "capital" of the Barbágia, the region's most notorious bandits are said to have taken refuge here in the first half of the 20th century, when the town averaged a murder every two months.

The Festa dell'Assunta takes place in Orgosolo on 15 August – a highlight of Barbágia and one of the top colourful processions of the region.

✚ 164 C3

Mural in Orgosolo

Where to... Stay

Prices

Expect to pay per double room, per night
€ under €90   €€ €90–€155   €€€ €155–€250   €€€€ over €250

GOLFO DI OROSEI

Hotel Su Barchile €€

This very welcoming 3-star hotel has ten rooms housed in a former dairy. It is modern and very comfortable and all rooms are air-conditioned. It also has a very good, highly regarded restaurant (▶ 96).

➕ 165 E4 🖾 Via Mannu 5, Orosei
☎ 0784 98879; www.subarchile.it

Hotel Costa Dorada €€–€€€

Set between the mountains and sea in this charming resort, this family-run small hotel is a little jewel set among flower-filled gardens. There are 23 comfortable rooms decorated in traditional Sardinian style and a vine-shaded dining terrace with splendid views over the Gulf of Orosei. The beach is across a small road from the hotel and there are many excursions on offer. In season, it also has exclusive use of The Marlin – a 55-foot boat (extra cost) to reach the hidden coves and beaches of the Gulf.

➕ 165 E4 🖾 Lungomare Palmasera 45, Cala Gonone ☎ 0784 93332;
www.hotelcostadorada.it 🕒 Apr–Oct

Hotel Pop €–€€

Just opposite the port, this friendly and welcoming 3-star hotel is a meeting point for the locals. Run by the charismatic Anglophile Simone Spanu and his family, service is excellent, rooms are modern and clean and every kind of excursion can be arranged. There is a lovely terrace outside overlooking the boats. It also has one of the resort's best restaurants, Al Porto (▶ 96).

➕ 165 E4 🖾 Via Marco Polo 2, Cala Gonone ☎ 0784 93185

Hotel Il Querceto €

Located on the southwestern side of the town, this 3-star property is in the typical mountain style. Rooms are airy and quite spacious and all overlook woodland from their balconies. The gardens are attractive and there are tennis courts.

➕ 165 D4 🖾 Via Lamarmora 4, Dorgali ☎ 0784 96509;
www.ilquerceto.com 🕒 Apr–Oct

OLIENA

Hotel Su Gologone €€€

Located 7km (4 miles) northeast of Oliena amid magnificent scenery, perched like a balcony on the Valle di Lanaittu, this is one of Sardinia's most lovely hotels/restaurants. There are 68 rooms and suites, decorated in harmony with the arts and crafts of the region. Most have a balcony. There is a swimming pool, beauty and relaxation centre and 4x4 excursions on offer. The restaurant is also very highly acclaimed (▶ 97).

➕ 164 C4 🖾 Località Su Gologone
☎ 0784 287512; www.sugologone.it
🕒 Mid-Mar–5 Nov

MONTE ORTOBENE

Fratelli Sacchi €–€€

Near the top of Monte Ortobene, this is a good base for immersing yourself in great views of the countryside. There are 22 comfortable, clean rooms that are rustic and a little old-fashioned; some have balconies. The restaurant specialises in local Nuorese cuisine and pizzas.

➕ 164 C4 🖾 Monte Ortobene
☎ 0784 31200; fax 0784 34030
🕒 Apr–Oct

Where to...
Eat and Drink

Prices

Expect to pay for a three-course meal for one, excluding drinks and service

€ under €26   €€ €26–€55   €€€ over €55

NÚORO

Bar Majore €

Something of an institution, this is Núoro's oldest café. The opulent interior has a frescoed ceiling, gilded stucco and antiques. It's a great place for immersing yourself in the local atmosphere.

➕ 164 C4 ⊠ Corso Garibaldi 71

Il Rifugio €–€€

Close to Madonna delle Grazie, this bustling trattoria/pizzeria is very popular with the locals. Home-made pasta and pizza are specialities and the pizza makers (*pizzaioli*) are

an entertainment in themselves.

➕ 164 C4 ⊠ Via Antonio Mereu 28/36 ☎ 0784 232355 🕐 Thu–Tue

GOLFO DI OROSEI

Ristorante Albergo Sant'Elene €€

Lying 3km (1.5 miles) off the SS125 from Dorgali, this restaurant is perched on a hillside. From the terrace there are glorious views, and the typical regional cuisine is no less splendid. Roast suckling pig, lamb, sea bass and appetisers of homemade paté are complemented by good wine and friendly service.

There are also excellent pizzas.

➕ 165 D4 ⊠ Località Sant'Elene, Dorgali ☎ 0784 94572 🕐 Summer daily; winter Tue–Sun; closed Jan

Ristorante Al Porto €€

Feast on local delicacies in the locals' favourite restaurant overlooking the port. Host Simone Spanu, affectionately known as Pop, is infectious in his enthusiasm for seafood – fishermen call him as they approach the dock to advise him of the catch of the day. Swordfish, octopus, succulent king prawns and puppy-sized lobsters all feature regularly, along with "Sardinian caviar" (*bottarga*), here served to perfection with spaghetti. There are also meat dishes.

➕ 165 E4 ⊠ Hotel Pop, Via Marco Polo 2, Cala Gonone ☎ 078 493185; www.hotelpop.com

Su Barchile €€

This very good restaurant, part of the hotel, prides itself on the traditions of the sea and land combined

in natural flavours. Carnivores are well catered for in dishes such as *porcetto* with myrtle, but the real emphasis is on fish and seafood, with over 44 dishes on the menu covering everything from spaghetti with lobster to plain, grilled, fresh fish. Try the delicious puddings and pastries served with the establishment's own *moscato* – dessert wine. The lovely outdoor terrace is perfect for summer dining.

➕ 165 E4 ⊠ Via Mannu 5, Orosei ☎ 0784 98879

Bue Marino €€–€€€

The terrace restaurant has glorious views of the entire Gulf of Orosei. Among the national and regional dishes, the specialities are fish and local desserts.

➕ 165 E4 ⊠ Via Vespucci 8, Cala Gonone ☎ 0784 920078 🕐 Mar–Jan

Colibrì €€

This warm and welcoming family-run restaurant specialises in traditional Sardinian cuisine such as

options and menus for children.
There is also an *à la carte* menu.
⊞ 165 E4 ⊠ Grotta di Ispinigoli
☎ 0784 95268;
www.hotelispinigoli.com

ORGOSOLO

Restaurant/Hotel Ai Monti del Gennargentu €€

Lying 5km (3 miles) from Orgosolo,
this pleasant rustic restaurant with
rooms, set among oak trees, is well
placed for discovering the local
mountain sights. The restaurant
specialises in traditional mountain
food, based on Sardinian meats.
⊞ 164 C3 ⊠ Località Settiles
☎ 0784 402374

Bar Podda €

This is a locals' hang out but prices
are very reasonable and it's as good
a place as any to get the local
flavour of Orgosolo. Usefully, it is
also an internet bar.
⊞ 164 C3 ⊠ Via Nuoro 7 ☎ 0784
402165

---

cinghiale (wild boar) and *porceddu*
(suckling pig). It also has very good
fish dishes.
⊞ 165 D4 ⊠ Via Gramsci 14 (corner
of Via Floris), Dorgali ☎ 0784 96054
☺ Jul–Aug daily; Sep–Jun Mon–Sat

Costa Dorada €€

The vine-shaded terrace restaurant
of this pretty, family-run hotel overlooks the Gulf of Orosei. On offer
are fresh catch of the day fish
specials as well as meat, all inspired
by traditional Sard recipes.
⊞ 165 E4 ⊠ Lungomare Palmasera
45, Cala Gonone ☎ 0784 493332
☺ Apr–Oct

Da Filippo Pizzeria €

More than 100 different types of
pizza are on offer at this friendly,
popular pizzeria. The Oroseina
has cream of aubergines, and
other typical offerings include the
Gennargentu, with local pecorino
cheese and mushrooms, and the
Nuragica, with ricotta and honey.
At lunchtime there is also a *menu*

---

del giorno, with *antipasti di terra e
mare* (meat, cheese and seafood).
Children's menus are also available,
including mouse-shaped Topolino
pizzas.
⊞ 165 E4 ⊠ Via Nazionale 195,
Orosei ☎ 0784 998159

OLIENA

Su Gologone €€€

This popular restaurant serves
Sardinian cuisine based on recipes
handed down through generations.
Delicious antipasti and home-made
pasta as well as the speciality
porceddu feature. There is a vast
wine cellar and local Oliena fine
wines are, as always, a treat. In
summer, dine on the outdoor
terrace admiring the glorious views.
⊞ 164 C4 ⊠ Hotel Su Gologone,
Località Su Gologone ☎ 0784
287512; www.sugologone.it

Ristorante Masiloghi €€

Located a little way out of town to
the east, this is a very good rustic

---

restaurant with tables spilling out
onto a verandah. Specials include
maccarrones a bocciu (handmade
Sardinian gnocchi) and *malloreddus*
(ravioli stuffed with sheep cheese or
ricotta). For main courses, meat is
the master, with spit-roasted or
barbecued pork, kid, lamb and wild
boar seasoned with aromatic herbs.
A good wine list is complemented
by myrtle liqueur or the famous
marc grappa (*fil'e ferru*). Gourmet
tasting menus are also available.
⊞ 164 C4 ⊠ Via Galiani 68, Oliena
☎ 0784 285696

GROTTA DI ISPINIGOLI

Hotel/Restaurant Ispinigoli
€–€€

Very conveniently located below the
entrance to the grotto, the
panoramic restaurant terrace is a
good place to relax while waiting
for a tour of the grotto that departs
on the hour. All tastes are catered
to, with set menus for vegetarians,
fish/seafood or traditional meat

Where to...
Shop

In Núoro there is an **ISOLA** outlet – a guarantee of authentic handmade crafts – at Corso Garibaldi 58 (tel: 078 433581; Mon–Sat 9–1, 4–8). For gourmet delicacies in Núoro visit **Tavola degli Antichi** at Via Trieste 70 (tel: 078 43501). Specialities available here from the Barbagia include *aranzada di Núoro* (candied orange peel and honey), and almond biscuits known as *s'aranzata*.

In Dorgali you will find **Esca Dolciaria** (Viale Kennedy, tel: 0784 94472), an excellent family-run pastries shop specialising in gourmet sweet delights, ranging from typical pastries of the Dorgali region to more traditional Sard confections.

Where to...
Be Entertained

ACTIVITIES

The area around Núoro is very scenic, hilly and untamed. The environment is host to many species of birds, from game to birds of prey. Following the old shepherds' trails, you walk in the tracks of wild boar, weasels, martens and foxes. The mountains around Oliena are full of grottos and passageways where there are superb opportunities for climbing and canyoning. For excursions including trekking, cross-country driving, canyoning, mountainbiking, caving, archaeology and diving, contact **Consortium Atlantika** (Via Lamarmora 195, Dorgali, tel: 328 972 9719). For quad biking, contact **Barbagia Insolita** (Corso Vittorio Emanuele 48, Oliena, tel: 0784 2860).

If you want to explore the coast alone, you can hire a **motorboat** in Cala Gonone from one of the companies that has kiosks on the harbour front. You can also hire RIBs (rubber inflatable fast boats) at **Malu** (tel: 348 765 3503/349 878 3317).

Cala Gonone is also a good centre for **diving** and there are several clubs such as the Argonauta, Via dei Lecci 10 (tel: 0784 93046; www.argonauta.it). On offer are guided snorkelling tours accompanied by professional guides; dives on World War II wrecks, caverns, and shallow dives and all levels of PADI dive courses. Specialities also include night diving.

NIGHTLIFE

Nightlife is fairly limited in this part of the island. There are a few bars in Núoro and one club, the **Boca Chica**, at Via Mughina 94 (tel: 329 312 0010) which has a Mexican theme and plays Latino-style music.

Cala Gonone becomes very lively in summer, with several discos alongside the Spiaggia Palmasera on the southern end. There are several bars, too, such as the **Roadhouse Blues** (Lungomare Palmasera) on the seafront and the popular cocktail bar of the Hotel Bue Marino (Via Vespucci 8, ▶ 96). Just out of town the summer disco **Lo Skrittiore** (Localita Iscrittiore, tel: 339 3303708) has a wide range of music from chart hits to Latin American sounds.

Monte Ortobene has a couple of bars that have events in summer, and is a very pleasant place to while away a few hours.

Sássari and the Northwest

Getting Your Bearings

The northwest has a different character from the rest of the island. It also has pretty seaside resorts, some of the island's best beaches, fine churches, nature reserves, countryside littered with *nuraghi*, Sardinia's second city and a very picturesque seaside Catalan city. But it is generally less rural, and, in places, is more reminiscent of the Italian mainland and of Spain.

The northern corner has the Parco Nazionale dell'Asinara, a nature reserve that is home to rare miniature albino donkeys. The jumping-off point for the island is the little seaside resort of Stintino, with the nearby Spiaggia della Pelosa – one of the island's most beautiful beaches with flour-white sand and crystalline, turquoise waters. Nearby Porto Tórres is a blot on the landscape with its petrochemical works and oil refinery and few vestiges of its former glory as the principal Roman port. However, the main Carlo Felice highway conveniently links this salty port to the rest of the island and to Stintino, and the handsome Pisan Basilica di San Gavino, Sardinia's largest Romanesque church, is worth investigating.

Inland Sássari is a vibrant university town with a lovely old medieval quarter and is second only to the capital, Cágliari. Alghero, too, has a tangle of medieval alleys and sits proudly at the head of the Riviera del Corallo (Coral Riviera) and has beautiful beaches. From here there's easy access by boat to Neptune's Grotto (Grotta di Nettuno), one of Sardinia's top sights. The scenic coastal drive south to the pretty riverside town of Bosa is sprinkled with beaches off the road, while inland lies "The Way of the Churches", the Valle dei Nuraghi and Nuraghe Santu Antíne, one of Sardinia's biggest and best *nuraghe*.

Page 99: Detail of carving on the Duomo di San Nicola façade, Sássari
Below: Porticoed entrance to Sanna Museum, Sássari
Opposite: Spiaggia della Pelosa

★ Don't Miss

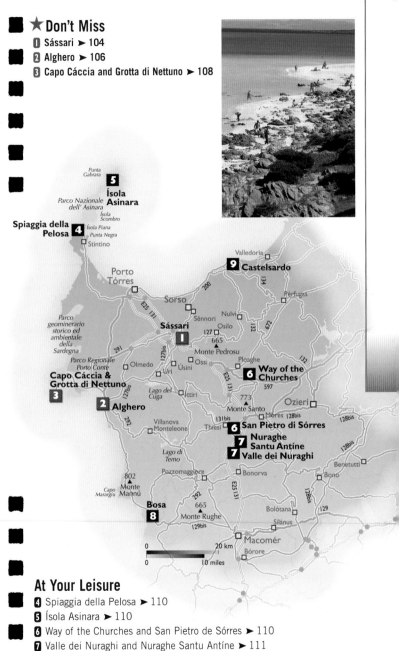

At Your Leisure

Sássari and the Northwest in Three Days

Day One

Morning

Travel to – or wake up in – **1** Sássari (➤ 104). Visit the compact old town and, at its heart, the baroque Duomo on its eponymous piazza. A short walk southwards to Piazza S Maria brings you to Santa Maria di Betlem and the massive wooden candles, *candelieri*. Have coffee at Florian, Via Roma. Pick your way round the Piazza Italia (under restoration) and cross into Corso Vittorio Emanuele II. Browse around the shops and marvel at the Teatro Cívico.

Lunch

Have lunch at Liberty/Piano Bar (➤ 114).

Afternoon

From Sássari drive 36km (22 miles) to **2** Alghero (below; ➤ 106). Head for the beach – Spiaggia Le Bombarde, west of Fertilia is the best. Walk around the *centro storico* and visit the excellent tourist office. Have a drink at the Café Latino (➤ 115) overlooking the port. Enjoy the shops and evening *passeggiata*, then have dinner at Angedras Restaurant, with views over the harbour (➤ 114).

Day Two

Morning

Drive from Alghero along the Riviera del Corallo past the curious town of Fertilia, laid out in rigid grid-system by Mussolini, past the lovely Porto Conte bay to Capo Cáccia. Visit the **3** Grotta di Nettuno (➤ 108). Have a welcome drink at the bar at the top of the steps. Drive northwest on the superstrada SS131 Carlo Felice highway bypassing Porto Tórres to **4** Spiaggia della Pelosa (➤ 110), just north of Stintino.

Lunch

Have lunch in Stintino at The Skipper or the beach bar I Genepi at La Pelosa (serves snacks all day and has musical evenings).

Afternoon

Drive east to **9** Castelsardo (➤ 112). Stroll through the tangle of little lanes leading up to the Castello and stay the night. (Alternatively, spend the night in Stintino and take the full-day excursion to **5** Ísola Asinara (➤ 110) the following morning.)

Day Three

Morning

Drive south to **6** San Pietro de Sórres (➤ 111) and nearby **7** Nuraghe Santu Antíne (➤ 111). Have coffee at the bar at the entrance to the *nuraghe* site. Drive west to Bosa.

Lunch

The best options are in Bosa.

Afternoon

Take the scenic coast road (above) from **8** Bosa to Alghero (➤ 112), stopping off to admire the views and visiting the little beaches. Overnight in Alghero.

⬛ Sássari

After Cágliari, this is Sardinia's second city – although the Sassarese will tell you that it is the first. It is sophisticated, cheerful, has a thriving café society and a fascinating *centro storico*, or historical centre. National politicians such as Antonio Segni, Francesco Cossiga and Enrico Berlinguer have been nurtured here in this, Sardinia's oldest university town.

The Medieval Town

At the core of the *centro storico*, the 15th-century **Duomo di San Nicola** has a baroque fantasy façade, added in the 18th century, very reminiscent of Puglian baroque you can see in Lecce in the south of Italy. The interior is by comparison very bare, although it does contain works of art such as the *Madonna con Bambino* by a 16th-century Sardinian artist, which adorns the high altar, and the walnut choirstalls.

Around here the lively narrow streets of the old medieval town are perfect for a stroll. Inevitably you end up at the **Corso Vittorio Emanuele II**. This street is full of *palazzi*, gorgeous wrought-iron balconies and handsome buildings – all in different states of neglect or, more recently, restoration. The lovely Liberty-style **Teatro Cívico** has been beautifully restored and the jewel-box interior is like a miniature version of Milan's La Scala.

Elaborate façade of San Nicola

North of here, along Corso Trinità, are remnants of the city's **medieval walls**, while the nearby **Fontana di Rosello** is a splendid Renaissance fountain sculpted in marble and dark stone. At each side there are statues of the four seasons with four white dolphin mouth spouts and eight lion-head spouts.

At Piazza di Santa Maria, close to the site of the original city walls, is the **Chiesa di Santa Maria di Betlem**. Founded in 1106, it has a lovely Romanesque façade, while the inside

Palazzo della
Provincia on
Piazza Italia,
Sássari's
grandest
square

is more overblown baroque. The lateral chapels display the
candelieri (giant wooden candles) that represent the town's
medieval craft guilds and are paraded for the 14 August festival. Made from wood and polychrome, they average around
420cm (160 inches) in height and weigh 310kg (685lb).

Around Piazza Italia

All roads lead to the heart of town on the **Piazza Italia**; this
is a building site at present, due to reopen in 2009. But a
stroll along the **Via Roma** just off the Piazza is always a
delight, and this is the centre of Sássari's thriving café society.

TAKING A BREAK

Enjoy a drink at **Florian** just off Piazza Italia (▶ 114).

🔲 158 C4

Duomo di San Nicola
🖂 Piazza Duomo 🕐 Open daily 9–12, 4–7 🎟 Free

Chiesa di Santa Maria di Betlem
🖂 Piazza di Santa Maria 🕐 Daily 7:15–12, 5–8

SÁSSARI: INSIDE INFO

In more depth Up to 12 men carry one *candeliero* in the **I Candelieri festival**.
Local dignitaries watch from the balcony of the Teatro Cívico; they clap if they
like the decoration of the giant candlesticks and boo if they don't.

One to miss Near the Duomo is, arguably, the ugliest square in Sardinia –
Piazza Mazzotti, once a notorious red-light area that was demolished to create a
soulless area; its saving grace is a very good pizzeria, da Bruno (▶ 114).

2 Alghero

A sign greets you to this picturesque walled medieval town with "Welcome to Alghero, the 'Riviera del Corallo'". Bathed in a warm coral glow, it sits on a little peninsula surrounded by towers and fortifications. This is both tourist town and fishing port and the lovely old centre has a tangle of narrow lanes filled with bars, restaurants and shops. It also has a distinct Catalan character as a result of Spanish colonisation in the 14th century.

Exploring the Old Town

The best place to start is at the excellent tourist information centre in Piazza Porta Terra, the old main entrance to the city. Nearby is the **Torre di Porta Terra**, a multimedia museum and panoramic terrace from where there are great views of the town and majolica dome of the **Chiesa di San Michele**.

The stone streets of the old city, narrow and lined with shops, are dotted with randomly spaced tiny piazzas. Elegant Spanish-style arches bridge the streets, festooned with laundry. The shops are decorated with coral jewellery and carvings, for which the town is famous.

The busiest lane in the Old Town is the **Via Carlo Alberto**, studded with shops and bars. But for less sybaritic interest there are the two churches – **San Michele** and **San Francesco**. The former dominates the skyline with its glistening ceramic dome and is perhaps the most opulent of the Jesuits' baroque churches on the island. The interior is full of sumptuous stucco and there are also fine altar paintings. San Francesco, halfway along the Via Carlo Alberto, is another of Alghero's landmarks, with its stately, pointed Aragonese tower. On summer evenings concerts are staged here.

Boats moored in Alghero's harbour

Alghero's other famous ecclesiastical landmark is the **Cattedrale**. Four large columns flank the white neoclassical façade. The interior is a mixture of architectural styles, but the impressive dome dates from the 18th century.

The Waterfront

The waterfront is girded by the *bastoni* (walls), and a walk along here makes a perfect evening *passeggiata*. The beaches in the immediate area have fine, white sand, but seaweed can sometimes be a problem: Alghero derives its name from the abundance of seaweed (*alghe*) in the surrounding waters. The best beaches are north of the town and the Lido on the way to Fertilia.

Parts of the cloister in San Francesco church date back to the 13th century

TAKING A BREAK

Have an aperitivo or lunchtime snack at **Il Ghiotto** (di Roberto Peana) in Piazza Cívica (► 114).

➕ 158 B3

Torre di Porta Terra
➕ 170 C2 ✉ Piazza Porta Terra ☎ 079 973 4045 🕐 Summer daily 9–1, 5–9 💰 Inexpensive ❓ Display panels are in Italian only

Chiesa di San Michele
➕ 170 B1 ✉ Via Carlo Alberto 🕐 Daily from 20 minutes before Mass

Chiesa di San Francesco
➕ 170 B2 ✉ Via Carlo Alberto 🕐 Mon–Sat 9:30–noon, 5–7:30, Sun 5–7:30

Cattedrale
➕ 170 B2 ✉ Piazza Duomo 🕐 Daily 7–12, 5–7:30. Campanile Tue, Thu, Sat 7–9:30pm; at other times call 079 973 3041

ALGHERO: INSIDE INFO

Top tips The **Sella & Mosca Vineyard**, outside town close to the airport, produces some of the island's top-quality wines. There are free guided tours daily plus the chance to buy from the shop (tel: 079 997700; Jun–Sep).

3 Capo Cáccia and Grotta di Nettuno

One of the top sights on the whole island is just to the west of Alghero. The limestone rock of the Capo Cáccia promontory has been buffeted and sculpted by wave and wind for 135 million years. From the lookout point there are glorious views over the cape and Ísola Foradada, while around the headland is the spectacular, giddying Escala del Cabirol (literally "goat's steps" in Catalan). This 654-step descent leads to the famous Grotta di Nettuno.

The stunning deep cavern with a lake is known as **Neptune's Grotto**, the mythical abode of nymphs. It is filled with stalactites and stalagmites twisted into fantastical shapes – a subterranean fairyland populated by shapes resembling human beings, statues, trees and animals. All is bathed in colour ranging from greenish-blue to white, yellow and orange crystals from the shimmering phosphorescence of the rock.

A tour of the Grotto takes you 200m (220 yards) around the shores of a saltwater lake, Lamarmora, facing the Acquasantiera – or holy water font – a huge 2m-high (6.5-foot) stalagmite. As the natural light ends and the darkness begins, shapes such as the Great Organ eerily seem to come to life. Guides fondly remember when visitors could row across the lake, lit by thousands of small candles on small plates floated on the water, creating an otherworldly glow of enchantment in the grand chamber. Let your imagination run free with the enchanting spectacle of those tiny, quivering

Steps lead past the limestone formations in the Grotta di Nettuno

The steps down to the cave cling to the sheer cliff face

flames throwing shadows on the wall and the reflections in the still waters of the lake.

Getting There

There are two ways to reach the Grotta from Alghero. By sea, a boat trip from the town port takes about an hour to get there. You pass by the Cape Galera and Punto Giglio cliffs, then round the tip of Capo Cáccia to arrive at the mouth of the caves lying at the foot of a towering cliff – a hugely impressive sight.

Overland by car, the caves are 24km (15 miles) from Alghero. The panoramic road (SS127) curves around Capo Cáccia, unfurling one of Sardinia's best views, taking in the bay of Porto Conte, Alghero itself, and stretching as far south as the Bosa coastline. There is a car park at Capo Cáccia.

TAKE A BREAK

At the top of the steps leading down to the Grotta di Nettuno there is a **bar** serving refreshing drinks and ice creams.

🚩 158 A3 ✉ Capo Cáccia ☎ 079 946540 🕐 Guided tours every hour Apr–Sep daily 9–7pm; Oct 9–5; Jan–Mar, Nov–Dec 9–4 💰 Expensive 🚢 Jun–Sep from Alghero 9:15, 3:10, 5:10; from Capo Cáccia noon, 4:05, 6:05pm; Oct–May 9:15 and noon departures only

CAPO DI CÁCCIA AND GROTTA DI NETTUNO: INSIDE INFO

Top tips Tours of the cave go on the hour – so try to time it so you don't have to hang around. They last 45 minutes and are led single-file by guides.

• The **Escala del Cabirol** is steep and not suitable for anyone suffering from vertigo. It takes around 15 minutes to make the descent – rather longer on the way back up.

• The **waves** around Capo Cáccia can become very high, and in rough weather the grotto is closed. However, if you go by boat there will be a stop instead in the lovely bay of Porto Conte, where you can have a dip in the sea.

At Your Leisure

❹ Spiaggia della Pelosa

This is one of the island's most beautiful beaches, with flour-fine white sand, lapped by clearest, shallow water in every shade of turquoise. It is guarded by a Spanish watchtower, Torre Falcone, on its own little islet on the northern side. The fine, soft sand dunes contrast perfectly with the dark rocks of the Capo Falcone peninsula at the back of the beach.

The beach lies 2km (1mile) north of Stintino by the Capo Falcone, the northwesternmost point of Sardinia. There is a fee for parking during summer, and it gets full quickly in July and August.

✚ 158 A5

❺ Ísola Asinara

"Donkey Island" became a national park in 1997, but its chequered history includes use as a maximum

La Pelosa beach

security penal centre until the 1970s. It takes its name from the island's unique population of miniature albino donkeys, who, along with pigs and mouflons (wild sheep), are its only inhabitants. The sea is cobalt blue and shallow, the white sandy beaches are beautiful – and they are not crowded as access is only possible on authorised excursions from Stintino. Transport is by bus, road train (*trenino*) or four-wheel drive, but you will need to bring your own refreshments.

✚ 158 A2 (inset)

❻ Way of the Churches and San Pietro de Sórres

The Logudoro (literally "place of gold") south and east of Sássari is lovely, rolling countryside, dotted with Romanesque churches left by the Pisans; the SS597, branching off towards Ólbia, is known as the "Way of the Churches". About 16km

(10 miles) southeast of Sássari, the 12th-century Basilica della SS Trinità di Saccargia dominates the countryside – a near-perfect example of Pisan Romanesque style. Dark volcanic basalt contrasts with light limestone stripes and its campanile soars 40m (130 feet). Other churches line the route, then some 16km (10 miles) farther east, perched majestically on a rocky outcrop, you come to Sant' Antíoco di Bisarcio. Dating from the 11th century and combining both Pisan and French influences, it is still grandiose although its campanile – built like a castle keep – has been gravely damaged by lightning.

Farther south, off the SS131, the striped white limestone and black trachyte façade of San Pietro de Sórres, one of Sardinia's best preserved Romanesque churches, overlooks the Valley of the Nuraghi (➤ below). In its grounds Benedictine monks restore old books and manuscripts in their workshop.

Basilica della SS Trinità di Saccargia
🗺 159 D3 🕐 Apr–Oct daily 9–dusk
💶 Inexpensive

Sant'Antíoco di Bisarcio
🗺 159 E3 🕐 Daily 9–1, 4–7 (but variable) 💶 Inexpensive

San Pietro de Sórres
🗺 159 D2 🕐 Daily 9:30–noon, 3:30–7:30

7 Valle dei Nuraghi and Nuraghe Santu Antíne

Torralba is at the head of the Valle dei Nuraghi (Valley of the Nuraghi), some 30km (19 miles) south of Sássari. The valley is strewn with ancient complexes, but the biggest is the Nuraghe Santu Antine. The central dry-stone tower made of basalt blocks towers up to 17m (56 feet) high. It was much higher, perhaps up to 21m (69 feet), when it was built, in around 1500BC, but it was partially demolished in the 19th century to build the village well in Torralba with (sacrilege!) modern mortar. Three later, smaller towers surround the compound linked by trenches and corridors. A spiral ramp leads up to the central tower's higher rooms. Possibly prehistoric burial chambers, they were converted by the Romans into a fortress and then transformed into a royal palace, known as "Sa Domo de Su Rei", by the early Christians.

Nuraghe Santu Antíne
🗺 159 E2 ✉ About 4km (2.5 miles) south of Torralba 🕐 Apr–Oct daily 9–dusk; Nov–Mar 9–5 💶 Moderate

Church of San Pietro de Sórres

Its fortunes seem to be on the upward spiral again, and many of the houses have recently been lovingly restored.

➕ 158 C7

Castello Malaspina and Chiesa di Nostra Signora di Regnos Altos

☎ 0785 373286 ⏰ Under continuing restoration so opening times variable

🔟 Bosa

The SP105 from Alghero to Bosa is a gloriously undulating stretch of 42km (26 miles) of coastal road, skirting little coves and swathes of golden-white sands before arriving at Bosa. This charming little town is clustered around the banks of the River Temo, crossed by the Ponte Vecchio bridge. There is a castle standing sentinel over the town, a cathedral and a medieval quarter, Sa Costa, with a fascinating tangle of alleys. The castle chapel, Nostra Signora di Regnos Altos, contains a wonderful 14th-century fresco cycle of famous saints. This ancient town was founded by the Carthaginians and was very prosperous until the 16th century.

🔟 Castelsardo

The imposing medieval citadel of Castelsardo perches on a rocky outcrop with a jumble of houses at its feet. Known in the 12th century as Castelgenovese, by the mid-15th century it had become Castelaragonese; its strategic importance has long since disappeared but it is still a popular landmark. The main sights are in the Old Town up the steep steps and streets where, apart from the castle, the Cattedrale di Sant'Antonio Abate is worth a look. From the top of the castle there are splendid views – right across to Corsica, on a clear day. The town is known for its hand-icrafts, especially l'intreccio (straw-weaving) – there's a museum devoted to it in the castle – ceramics, cork and wooden masks.

➕ 159 D5

Cattedrale di Sant'Antonio Abate

⏰ Summer daily 7am–8pm; winter 7–5:30

Bosa shelters under its commandingly sited castle

Where to... Stay

Prices
Expect to pay per double room, per night
€ under €90   €€ €90–€155   €€€ €155–€250   €€€€ over €250

SÁSSARI

Casa Chiara €
In a side street near the university, this boho-style B&B occupies the second floor of an atmospheric old building. The three spacious rooms are brightly coloured and there are two shared bathrooms. Good breakfasts include multicoloured Sardinian pastries.

🚩 158 C4 ⊠ Vicolo Bertolinis 7 (Piazza Azuni) ☎ 079 200552; www.casachiara.net

Hotel Vittorio Emanuele €–€€
In the heart of the city, this pleasing former *palazzo* has been fully restored. The result is carefully furnished, comfortable rooms where style veers to modern minimalist, but not without murals. There is a good restaurant, Platha de Cothinas, and a rustic stone cellar – perfect for wine-tasting.

🚩 158 C4 ⊠ Corso Vittorio Emanuele II 100/102 ☎ 079 235538; fax: 079 200 6696; www.hotelvittorioemanuele.ss.it

ALGHERO

Hotel San Francesco €€
A former convent, this is Alghero's only hotel in the Old Town and a perfect retreat. The best rooms overlook the old cloisters of the Chiesa di San Francesco. Breakfast, which is included in the price, is savoured in the cloisters. There's no parking, but a nearby garage is available for €5 per night.

🚩 170 B2 ⊠ Via Ambrogio Machin 2 ☎ 079 980330; www.sanfrancescohotel.com

Agriturismo Vessus €
This family-run countryside hotel is an oasis set in olive groves and attractive gardens where the traditional-style rooms encircle the swimming pool. The very good restaurant specialises in traditional Sardinian food and includes home-grown fruit, vegetables and, of course, olives and olive oil. The restaurant is open only from June to September for dinner.

🚩 158 B2 ⊠ SS292 per Villanova Monteleone Km 1.85 (3km south of Alghero) ☎ 079 973 5018; www.vessus.it

Hotel Villa Las Tronas €€€€
Spectacularly located on a private promontory overlooking the sea, this former Italian royal family holiday home is Alghero's most luxurious hotel. Antiques, marbled halls, chandeliers and rich brocades ooze opulence in this 19th-century castellated pleasure palace. There is a saltwater swimming pool, beauty centre, gym and wellness centre.

🚩 158 B3 ⊠ Lungomare Valencia 1 ☎ 079 981818; fax: 079 981044; www.hotelvillalastronas.it

BOSA

Corte Fiorita €–€€
Made up of three different historical buildings, this collection of *albergi* is in the heart of Bosa. The rooms are rustic, light and spacious, with tiled floors, exposed stone walls and tasteful fabrics; those with balcony and river view charge a supplement. Breakfast can be taken in a walled courtyard at Le Palme, the check-in point for all properties.

🚩 158 C1 ⊠ Lungo Temo De Gasperi 45 ☎ 078 537 7058; fax: 078 537 2078; www.albergo-diffuso.it

Where to...
Eat and Drink

Prices

Expect to pay for a three-course meal for one, excluding drinks and service
€ under €26   €€ €26–€55   €€€ over €55

SÁSSARI

Ristorante Pizzeria da Bruno €

This excellent restaurant is the saving grace of the singularly ugly Piazza Mazzotti, where 1960s concrete meets medieval town. Good pizzas and pasta can be enjoyed on an outdoor terrace offering views towards the rooftops of the old town.

➕ 158 C4 ⊠ Piazza Mazzotti 12
☎ 079 235573

Florian €€

Elegantly mirrored and muralled, both Bar Caffè Florian and the next-door restaurant are good spots for dining. The bar has tables spilling out onto the pavement outside and Toulouse-Lautrec-style touches inside. A delicious *spremuta di arancia* (freshly squeezed blood orange juice) or cappuccino is excellent value. The restaurant is more expensive but very good.

➕ 158 C4 ⊠ Bar Caffè Florian, Via Roma 6 ⊠ Florian, Via Capitano Bellieni 27 ☎ 079 200 8056
☎ Mon–Sat

Ristorante Liberty €€

Set in a small piazza in the town centre, next to the Corso Vittorio Emanuele, this elegantly restored restaurant was a little Liberty-style *palazzo*. The speciality is fish. Inside you can choose between the Sala Afrodite or the Sala Apollo dining rooms, differentiated by their murals. Alongside is the atmospheric wine/piano bar with a stream running down the stone steps into the tasting cellar. This serves a good selection of snacks, including cheeses and cold cuts at €6 an item, to accompany your wine.

➕ 158 C4 ⊠ Piazza N Sauro 3
☎ 079 236361 ☎ Tue–Sun

Bar Ristorante Mokador €

This buzzing little place is popular with the locals and a good choice for inexpensive snacks and drinks. On Fridays there is Happy Hour 7–9pm, with *antipasti all'italiana* on offer for an all-inclusive price of €5.

➕ 158 C4 ⊠ Largo Cavallotti 2, off Piazza Castello, near Via Roma
☎ 079 235736

ALGHERO

Angedras Restaurant €€

Chef Alessandro Tesi prepares a short, well-chosen menu featuring seafood tasting plates (*degustazione di mare*), homemade pasta such as *spaghetti alla chitarra con vongole e fiori du zucca* (spaghetti with clams and courgette flowers), fresh fish and seafood and meat-based dishes, too. Traditional Sardinian puddings are delicious, and the *tortino al cioccolato con gelato alla banana* (dark chocolate flan with home-made banana ice cream) is sublime. Portions are more nouvelle cuisine than gargantuan in size in this new, minimalist-style restaurant. Outdoor seating overlooks the port and sunset.

➕ 170 A2 ⊠ Via Cavour 31, corner of Bastioni Marco Polo ☎ 079 073 5078

Il Ghiotto (di Roberto Peana) €

This "snackeria" specialises in *prodotti tipici* – cold cuts of meat and salami, cheeses, pizza, salads and sandwiches. There's a buffet lunch, but you can opt just to have an aperitivo and enjoy a free tasting of the various goodies. The attached shop has tempting displays of Sardinian specialities.

🚹 170 B2 ☒ Piazza Civica 23
☎ 079 974820 ⓒ Daily; lunch buffet 12:30–3:30

Café Latino €–€€

Overlooking the port, this is the perfect spot to chill out under the white parasols or inside among the cool stone vaults. Good snacks incude panini, pizzas and delicious icecreams. Alternatively, enjoy a long cool beer or cocktails while watching the boats and the world go by.

🚹 170 B2 ☒ Bastioni Magellano 10
☎ 079 976541 ⓒ Jul–Aug daily 9am–11pm; closed Tue Sep–Jun

Bella Napoli €–€€

Neapolitan owned pizzeria with generous portions and good pasta dishes as well as pizzas. Inside it's

lively, outside there's a parasol-shaded terrace. Good pasta dishes include ravioli with ricotta cheese and *penne alla siciliana* (spicy quill-shaped pasta).

🚹 170 B2 ☒ Piazza Civica 29
☎ 079 983014 ⓒ Thu–Tue

Trattoria Al Refettorio €€

Chic and atmospheric wine bar with excellent nibbles to accompany your aperitivo. The restaurant food is also good – and there is outdoor, covered seating. Fresh fish and seafood as well as dishes such as wild boar and other carnivorous delights feature. As you would expect, it has a very good, extensive wine list.

🚹 170 B2 ☒ Carreró del Porxo (Vicolo Adami) 47, off Via Roma
☎ 079 973 1126; www.alrefettorio.it
ⓒ Wed–Mon

STINTINO

Ristorante da Antonio €€

Set on a road back from the sea,

this welcoming family-run restaurant specialises in fish and seafood. The "music bread" (▶ 23, 38) is excellent and the grilled fresh tuna fish is sublime and goes especially well with the very good rosé Sella & Mosca wine from Alghero. Portions tend to be very generous and service is also very attentive.

🚹 158 B5 ☒ Via Marco Polo 16
☎ 079 523077

BOSA

Borgo Sant'Ignazio €€

Follow the signs through the tangle of alleys of the old town up to this atmospheric bistro. Specialities include local *aragosta* (lobster) as well as Sardinian meat specialities. Being on the *strada della malavasia di Bosa*, it also has a good selection of Malvasia dessert wines to accompany typical Sardinian sweetmeats.

🚹 158 C1 ☒ Via Sant'Ignazio 33
☎ 0785 374662 ⓒ Tue–Sun 1–3, 7:30–11

Sa Pischedda €€

Under the same ownership as the hotel of this name, this excellent restaurant is part of the Slow Food Movement. Prepare to linger over seasonal delicacies and Sardinian specialities and enjoy a glass of Malvasia wine with your pudding. Also run by the hotel is the Ponte Vecchio, on a jetty above the river, which specialises in seafood in a very romantic setting.

🚹 158 C1 ☒ Via Roma 8 ☎ 0785 373065 ⓒ Apr–Sep daily; Oct–Mar Wed–Mon

CASTELSARDO

La Guardiola €€

One of the town's top restaurants occupies the top location in the Old Town, just below the Castello. The speciality is seafood and there is a lovely dining terrace overlooking the sea.

🚹 159 D5 ☒ Piazza Bastione 4
☎ 079 470755 ⓒ Jun–Sep daily; Oct–May Tue–Sun

Where to...
Shop

In **Alghero** there is a wide range of boutiques for clothes, shoes and leather goods, plus shops selling locally crafted ceramics, pottery, cork and hand-woven baskets. There is also a huge choice of jewellery shops, mostly specialising in the local red coral, unique to this coastline. The modern side of town starts at **Via XX Settembre**, where there are larger shops, perfumeries and boutiques. There's a daily fresh fish, fruit and vegetable market in Via Sássari; a large street market on Wednesday morning and a collectors' market on the last Sunday in the month.

Bosa is at the centre of vineyards – the Strada della Malvasia di Bosa – and is famous especially for its Malvasia wine. For Sard handicrafts such as filigree work, coral, ceramics, traditional knives, embroidery and tablecloths, visit **Deriu** (Artiginiato Sardo e Souvenir) at Via Gioberti 14 (tel: 0785 375037).

In **Sássari** there are several markets, such as the covered market for fish (closed Mon), plus vegetables and meat. There's also a Sardinian handicrafts market in front of the Garibaldi Statue (closed Mon). **Bagella**, at Corso Vittorio Emanuele 20 (tel: 079 235033; www.bagella.it), one of Sássari's oldest shops, specialises in authentic traditional Sardinian clothing such as velvet suits, shirts, leather accessories and boots. The 15th-century Catalan Gothic **Casa di Rienzo** is now a Goldenpoint lingerie shop with stunning ceilings. **Mura** (di Elisabetta e Luisa Branca) at Via Roma 12 (tel: 079 235332) is a chic gift shop specialising in jewellery, silver, decorative objects and some antiques at a broad spectrum of prices.

Where to...
Be Entertained

In **Alghero**, the **Teatro Cívico** (tel: 079 997800) is in Piazza Vittorio Emanuele in the Old Town.

There is live music and bowling at **Poco Loco**, Via Gramsci 8 (tel: 079 973 1034), just off the main seafront promenade, Piazza Sulis. In high summer there are plenty of clubs and discos and the best place (currently) is south of the centre, along the Lungomare, but venues do tend to come and go. Just out of town, the **Ruscello** lies north on the Olmedo road and has open-air dancing and live bands (tel: 339 235 0755; Jul–Aug nightly).

Sássari has a thriving cultural scene with several theatres, including the **Teatro Cívico** in Corso Vittorio Emanuele (tel: 079 232182) and **Teatro Ferroviario** at Corso Vico 14 (tel: 079 263 3049). You can get information from the tourist office about what's on. As you would expect from a university town, there are plenty of good, buzzing bars, especially along the Via Roma and in Piazza Castello.

WATERSPORTS

For excursions from Stintino to the Parco Nazional dell'Asinara including Land Rover drives, contact the **Azienda Mare e Natura**, Via Sássari 77 (tel: 079 520097). For boat trips from Alghero aboard the sailing boat **Andrea Jensen**, including helping with steering and sail-rigging, swimming and snorkelling, contact 33390 708139; www.ajsailing.com.

The Northeast

Getting Your Bearings

Granite landscapes, fantastic formations of wind and sea-sculpted rock, prehistoric stone dwellings and a beautiful, more discrete coastline scattered with islands and indented with picturesque coves – this is Gallura. The sea around here really does sparkle like a jewel and the Costa Smeralda – "Emerald Coast" – is outdazzled only by the bejewelled and glamorous people who flock to this exclusive playground.

Planes, boats, trains and buses arrive at Ólbia, a convenient gateway to the pleasures of this beautiful region. But driving around the city can be very tedious, as it seems to be permanently under roadworks, so while it does have some good restaurants, it is not a place to linger long. From here there are regular boat trips to the imposing Ísola Tavolara, standing sentinel over the bay.

The fabled Costa Smeralda is within easy reach of Ólbia and the Pevero coastline has glorious white sandy beaches and turquoise seas. Nearby are resorts such as Cannigione and Santa Teresa di Gallura, which are less glitzy but still bask along beautiful stretches of coast.

Palau is the gateway to the seven islands of the Arcipélago de La Maddalena, where a highlight is Giuseppe Garibaldi's island, Caprera, where he lived and is buried.

The interior of the Gallura seems worlds apart from the pleasures of the beach. Arzachena is a true Sardinian town and worth visiting for its excellent prehistoric sites. And the old capital of Gallura, Témpio Pausánia, is an hour's drive away through beautiful countryside up into the mountains. You will come across lakes and waterfall walks on the way up to the highest peak, Monte Limbara. In this region of great contrasts, it is a delight to discover another side of Sardinia.

★ Don't Miss

Page 117:
Windsurfer off
Capo Testa
Opposite: The
Maddalena
islands are famous
for their rocky
shoreline
Below: Villa roofs
at Porto Cervo

Santa Teresa
di Gallura **6**
Capo Testa

Parco Nazionale
dell' Arcipélago
de La Maddalena **3**
Ísola Maddalena

La Maddalena

5 Ísola Caprera

Museo
Garibaldino

Palau

133bis

133

125

Vignola Mare
l'Agnata

Basscutena

4 Porto
Cervo

Arzachena **8**
Cannigione
Punta
Capaccia **2**

Costa
Smeralda

765
Serra di
lu Tassu

133

Lago di
Liscia

427

Porto Rotondo

Porto
Rotondo

Golfo
Aranci

Capo
Figari

125

Ággius
7

911
Punta Sálici

Lúras

Calangiánus

427

127

Monti Ultana

Ólbia
1

Golfo di
Ólbia

**Ísola
Tavolara**
1

7 Témpio
Pausánia

127

1359
Punta
Balestrieri

199

127

E840

131dcn

125

Riserva
Marina

Ísola
Molara

Capo
Coda
Cavallo

392

Lago del
Coghínas

Berchidda

199

Monti

389

Monti di Alá

389

Padru

Oschiri

597

199

1077
Punta di
Senalonga

926
Punta
sa Mesa

Ala dei Sardi

Altopiano
di Buddusò

1093
Pattada Monte Lerno

Lago
Lerna

Budduso

0 _____ 20 km

0 _____ 10 miles

At Your Leisure

The Northeast in Four Days

Day One

Morning
Arrive in **❶** Ólbia (right; ➤ 122). Walk up to the old part of town and the Corso Umberto. Take a look at the Basilica di San Simplicio (past the level crossing and railway station), then make your way to Porto San Paolo to take a boat trip to Ísola Tavolara.

Lunch
At Ristorante da Tonino on Ísola Tavolara (➤ 133). Spend the afternoon relaxing on the beach.

Afternoon
Return to Ólbia and, if time permits, travel to Cannigione to stay overnight. Enjoy dinner here, perhaps at l'Ancora (➤ 133), and make a visit to the night market, which is open during the summer season.

Day Two

Morning
Set off for the **❷** Costa Smeralda (➤ 124). Make your way to Porto Cervo. Admire the boats in the marina or do a spot of window shopping in the **❹** Piazzetta (right; ➤ 128).

Lunch
Explore the beaches and have lunch in Cala di Volpe at the very reasonably priced Bar Baretto Pizzeria, which serves really good pizzas and salads on an outdoor terrace.

Afternoon
Take a boat trip or relax on the beaches. Stay overnight in Palau or Santa Teresa.

Day Three

Morning
Set off to visit the ❸ Arcipélago de La Maddalena (► 126). There are regular ferries from Palau, which you can take as a foot passenger or with a car. Enjoy a stroll around the old town of La Maddalena and have a coffee in the Piazza Garibaldi and/or take a boat trip to the islands of the archipelago and have lunch on board.

Afternoon
Enjoy exploring the other islands, including Caprera (accessible also by road), perhaps with a visit to ❺ Garibaldi's home and museum (► 128). Return to the mainland.

Day Four

Morning
Set off for inland Gallura and head to ❻ Arzachena (► 129). Take a look at Il Fungo rock and then visit Coddu Vecchiu and the nearby Tomba dei Giganti di Li Lolghi and Necropoli di Li Muri. From here make your way to ❼ Témpio Pausánia (► 129).

Lunch
There are pleasant restaurants to choose from in Témpio Pausánia.

Afternoon
West of Témpio, the hill village ❼ Ággius (► 129) is a good place to visit for its handicrafts and Museo Etnográfico. Out of town to the north is the lunarscape of the Valle della Luna. Return to the coast.

❶ Ólbia and Ísola Tavolara

Ólbia's origins were Phoenician before the town became a Roman trading post, and today it is Sardinia's busiest passenger port. Few vestiges of its former glory remain but the Basilica di San Simplicio is Gallura's most important medieval church. The giant Tavolara rock towers over the bay – a favourite with peregrine falcons and one of the smallest kingdoms on the planet.

On arrival at Ólbia you could be forgiven for trying to get out of it as quickly as possible – it is busy, traffic-choked and full of roadworks. However, the cobbled lanes in the old part of town around **Corso Umberto** are full of good restaurants and pretty piazzas to linger in over a drink. From here, past the railway station, you come to the town's top sight, the **Basilica di San Simplicio**. This 11th–12th century Pisan Romanesque church is hewn out of Galluran granite. Inside there are columns and other pieces of masonry salvaged from Phoenician and Roman temples. In the apse there are two 13th-century frescoes, the left-hand one of which depicts San Simplicio, the patron saint of Ólbia.

Ísola Tavolara
Measuring a mere 4km long by 1km wide (2.5 by 0.5 miles), this island just to the south of Ólbia is dominated by its imposing rock towering over 564m (1,850 feet) high, and is part of a protected marine park. The eastern side of Tavolara is a military zone, but there's free access to the inhabited western side, which even has a cemetery. Here are the tombs of Tavolara's kings, as Tavolara, despite its size, is a kingdom.

When King Carlo Alberto of Sardinia visited the island in 1833 for a spot of goat hunting and feasting, he thanked his host, Giuseppe Bertoleoni, by "crowning" him as an independent sovereign monarch. Since then the island's "kings" have all descended from the Bertoleoni family; the present sovereign, Carlo II, runs the Da Tonino restaurant.

Wild goats still roam and it is a paradise for birds, including eagles and peregrine falcons. On the southern tip there's a good beach at **Spalmatore di Terra**.

Above: Café terrace in Piazza Margherita, Ólbia
Opposite: The austere but handsome façade of San Simplicio church

TAKING A BREAK
Dine like a king at **Tonino's** restaurant on Ísola Tavolara, run by the present monarch of the island (► 133).

🔲 Ólbia 161 D3, Ísola Tavolara 161 E3

ÓLBIA AND ÍSOLA TAVOLARA: INSIDE INFO

Top tips Ólbia's **Feast of San Simplicio** takes place on 15 May.
• Tavolara island hosts an open-air **film festival** of non-mainstream Italian films in mid-July for four or five nights, which are screened on the beach. For more information contact the Ólbia tourist office or visit www.cinematavolara.it

② Costa Smeralda

The waters of the Emerald Coast sparkle like a precious jewel, reflected in the diamonds and platinum of those who flock to this millionaires' playground. In the 1950s the Aga Khan fell in love with the sandy beaches and idyllic coves along this 10km (6-mile) coastal strip and made it an exclusive resort. But the charms of this coastline are not confined to the "Smeralda"; gorgeous beaches and bays are all around.

The Costa Smeralda begins around 12km (7.5 miles) north of Ólbia and extends just 10km (6 miles) between the Golfo di Cugnana and Golfo di Arzachena, but has a beautiful 56km (35-mile) coastline. The area has stuck firmly by the guiding principle that all development should blend into the superb scenery without disfiguring it in any way. So there are no high-rise buildings; telephone wires and electrical cables have to be hidden underground; and the buildings are a curious mix of troglodyte-Moroccan styles.

Porto Cervo

Porto Cervo is the only real town and "capital" of the area. Disguised as a Mediterranean fishing village, it's a pleasant place to stroll, to see and be seen – and to window shop (➤ 128). It all tends to be very quiet during the day as everyone is relaxing on their boat or villa or on the beach. The best time to visit is at sunset and later.

Other Resorts

The **Pevero** coastline that has made Sardinia so famous is lined with beaches and coves accessed by rough tracks off the road leading to Porto Cervo. West of the Cala di Volpe bay, Capriccioli and Romazzino beaches are good stopping points.

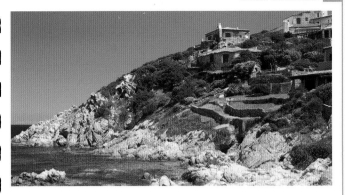

Above: Houses are dotted discreetly about the hillsides around Porto Cervo

Opposite: Coastline near Romazzino

On the eastern side of the Golfo di Cugnana is **Porto Rotondo**. It is a chi-chi resort with obligatory marina, and is the site of Silvio Berlusconi's 40-room Villa La Certosa (► 26). Not really part of the Costa Smeralda, having been built later, it also has beautiful beaches and is equally expensive to stay in.

To the south, the resort of **Golfo Aranci** lies on the tip of Capo Figari. This is more of a family resort, with lovely beaches helpfully numbered from one to five – the third of which, "La Terza Spiaggia", is the best.

Also within easy reach of Costa Smeralda is **Cannigione** in the Gulf of Arzachena – an attractive, lively village with a picturesque port and marina. You can still sport your Prada shades but you're not so likely to go over your credit limit here. The nearby headland, **Capo d'Orso**, is a huge, bear-shaped rock. It's 122m (400 feet) high and affords stunning views across to Corsica and the Maddalena islands.

TAKING A BREAK

L'Ancora at La Conia is a family-friendly restaurant just north of town in the hills. It serves everything from pasta to seafood.

✚ 161 E4

COSTA SMERALDA: INSIDE INFO

Top tips The **Porto Cervo marina** hosts many regattas and races, including the Settimana delle Bocche at the end of August, the Sardegna Cup for yachts and the Premio Offshore for powerboats.

• Borrow or rent a **boat** to reach all those hideaway coves and beaches.

Hidden gem The lovely beach **Portu Li Coggi** (or Spiaggia del Principe, the Prince's Beach), is poorly signposted, but is really worth a little effort. From Cala di Volpe, keep the famous hotel to the right while heading south for about 2.5km (1.5 miles). Before Capriccioli take the junction for Romazzino on the left. Head north and near the resort (1.4km/0.8 miles) take a right towards the sea. After about 300m (330 yards) downhill you come to a barrier preventing car access. From here a short mule track takes you to the shore.

③ Arcipélago de La Maddalena

Seven dreamy islands with Caribbean-blue seas make up the archipelago north of the Costa Smeralda. The only inhabited island is La Maddalena itself, from where there is a causeway to Garibaldi's island, Caprera. But there are boat trips to see the other islands, including Spargi and Budelli with its glorious pale pink beach, Spiaggia Rosa.

Rocks hewn over thousands of years characterise the landscape of the Gallura, and on La Maddalena there are about 150 of them whose shape has earned them nicknames such as Rabbit Rock, Eagle's Beak, De Gaulle, Dinosaur, and even Il Mostro di Lochness (Loch Ness Monster).

La Maddalena Town

The most popular way of getting to La Maddalena is by the 20-minute ferry crossing from Palau to La Maddalena town. This is a bustling place with cobbled streets and piazzas, and a decorous *passeggiata* along the Via Garibaldi, the main street that connects Piazza Umberto I to Piazza Garibaldi. There are also some good restaurants around the squares and pleasant bars in which to people-watch.

In terms of sights, there are few, but the **Museo Diocesano** has some fascinating exhibits, including gifts from Lord Horatio Nelson. The Commander of the British fleet made regular visits here aboard the *Victory* from 1803 to 1805 to keep an eye on the French fleet anchored in the port of Toulon. He struck up a good relationship with Agostino Millelire, Commander of the Port of La Maddalena, and on

Boats in the harbour at La Maddalena town

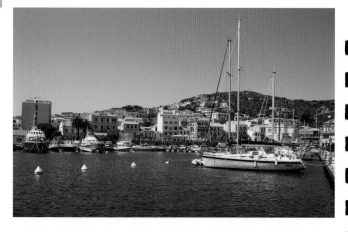

his departure, presented two silver candlesticks and a crucifix to the church, **Chiesa di S Maria Maddalena**. Proudly displayed in the museum with the silver "treasures" is Nelson's letter of 18 October 1804 thanking the inhabitants for their treatment of his fleet. There is also a huge display of *ex voto* gifts, including 500 rings, ranging from the very poor to the very, very rich.

Out of the centre on the road to Cala Spalmatore (about 1km/0.5 miles) you come to the **Museo Archeológico Navale** on Via Panoramica. The main exhibits are of a Roman cargo ship that was wrecked in the waters of the archipelago around 120BC, showing a reconstructed cross-section of the hull and amphorae, most of which contained wine.

La Caprera
To the east of the island a causeway links to pine-covered La Caprera. As well as visiting the Garibaldi museum (➤ 128), this is a pleasant place to walk or cycle around (➤ 147–148).

Beaches
The best beaches on La Maddalena are Cala Maiore Spiaggia di Bassa Trinità and Stagno Torto on the west coast and Cala Lunga on the northeast. On Caprera there are the Due Mari beaches in the south and, on the east, Cala Brigantino and Cala Colticcio. The other islands are reachable only by boat.

Rocky outcrops punctuate the beaches

TAKING A BREAK
Have a drink or snack at La Maddalena's **Osteria Enoteca da Liò**, Corso Vittorio Emanuele 2/6 (tel: 0789 737507).

➕ 161 D5 🚢 Regular ferries from Palau, and from Cannigione and Santa Teresa in season

Museo Diocesano
✉ Chiesa di S Maria Maddalena, Via Baron Manno ☎ 0789 737400 🕐 Tue–Sun 10–1, 3–8

Museo Archeológico Navale
✉ Via Panoramica ☎ 0789 790660 🕐 May–Sep Tue–Sun 10:30–12:30, 3:30–7; Oct–Apr 10:30–12:30

At Your Leisure

4 Porto Cervo's Piazzetta

The Piazzetta is full of cool archways, loggias, bars and shops. Members of the international jetset rub shoulders with tourists and there are numerous designer boutiques to drool over. All the usual suspects are here, including Bulgari, Dolce & Gabbana and Valentino – where a pair of shoes will set you back €1,000 at a conservative estimate. Overlooking the Piazzetta is the Cervo Hotel, whose piano bar and terrace are a favourite gathering place and a gorgeous spot to indulge in a sundowner. Try a *fragolino*, a delicious *aperitivo* of strawberries with vodka and sparkling wine.

➕ 161 D4

5 Garibaldi's Memorial Museum, Isola Caprera

Often likened to an Italian Che Guevara, the revolutionary Giuseppe Garibaldi (1807–82) made Caprera his home in 1855. It was his refuge after his campaigns in the pursuit of unification, and he found solace in the peace and wild nature of this island. In the courtyard stands a majestic pine planted by Garibaldi on the day his daughter Celia was born (he had seven children by three wives and one by a governess). The house, Casa Bianca, has changed little since his death. His personal effects include his trademark famous red shirt (*camicia rossa*), after which his troops – the Red Shirts – were named, and two embroidered fez hats. The rooms are small and simple, with the exception of his more spacious death chamber. Built at the request of his wife, Francesca, it looks out to the Straits of Bonifacio and towards Nice, the city of his birth. In this room the calendar shows the date of his death, Friday 2 June 1882. His tomb in the garden is made of rough granite, in total contrast with the grandiose marble tombs of five of his children and his last wife.

➕ 161 D5 ✉ Museo Garibaldino di Caprera 🕐 Jun–Sep Tue–Sun 9–1:30, 4–6:30; Oct–May 9–1:30 💶 Moderate

Garibaldi Museum on Ísola Caprera

Rena Bianca beach at Santa Teresa

6 Santa Teresa di Gallura

Lying on the northernmost tip of the
island, this is now a very popular
summer resort. From the main
Piazza Vittorio Emanuele, the Via del
Mare leads to the 16th-century
Spanish watchtower, Torre di
Langosardo. From here you can
drink in the glorious views over the
straits of Bonifacio to Corsica. A path
leads west of the tower to the main
beach, Spiaggia Rena Bianca. Ferries
leave daily for the 50-minute trip
across to Bonifacio on Corsica – a
great day out for a French lunch and
some shopping. There are also boat
trips to the Maddalena islands.

The granite headland, Capo Testa,
lies 4km (2.5 miles) to the west. It
has two beaches: the one on the left-
hand side has crystalline waters and
soft sand that shelves gently, while
the beach on the right has amazing
rock formations.

🔀 160 B5

Torre di Longosardo
🕐 Jun–Sep daily 10–12:30, 4–7
💶 Inexpensive

7 Témpio Pausánia and Ággius

Témpio Pausánia, in the heart of the
Gallura, lies at 550m (1,820 feet)

surrounded by dense forests of cork
oak. This granite hilltop town, joint
capital of the province of Ólbia-
Témpio, is a centre of cork manufac-
turing and wine production,
especially Vermentino. It is a town of
churches, the most important of
which is the 15th-century Cattedrale
di San Pietro, substantially rebuilt in
the 19th century. Next door, the
Oratorio del Rosario, built by the
Aragonese and rebuilt in the 18th
century, has an elaborate baroque
altar decorated with pure gold.

Lying 10km (6 miles) west of
Témpio, the hill village Ággius is
famous for its handicrafts, especially
woven carpets. The Museo
Etnográfico gives a fascinating
insight into this craft and traditions
of inland Gallura. North of here you
come to the Valle della Luna (Valley
of the Moon) – a lunar landscape
where enormous granite rocks rise
out of the ground in fantastic,
contorted shapes.

🔀 160 B3

Museo Etnográfico
✉ Via Monti di Lizu ☎ 079 621029;
www.aggius.net 🕐 Mid-May to mid-Oct
daily 10–1, 4–8:30; mid-Oct to mid-May
Tue–Sun 10–1, 3:30–7

8 Arzachena Prehistoric Sites

Away from the coast, discover giants'
tombs and megalithic stone circles in
the prehistoric remains dotted in the
woods and fields around Arzachena,

about half an hour's drive from Ólbia. Among olive groves, myrtle and prickly pear, the Nuraghe Albucciu, 2km (1 mile) southeast of the town, is one of Gallura's best-preserved *nuraghi*. It has an unusual granite roof that is flat rather than conical. About 4km (2.5 miles) south of Arzachena is Coddu Vecchiu, one of the island's most complete "giants' tombs". The original corridor tomb is estimated to date to the 18th–16th centuries BC, then extended in Nuraghic times by adding a forecourt edged by stone.

Nearby are the Tomba dei Giganti di Li Lolghi and Necropoli di Li Muri. Li Lolghi rises on a hillock and, although similar to Coddu Vecchiu, is nearly twice as long in the inner chamber. The necropolis of Li Muri is reached by returning on the rough track to the left fork going west off the track from the road sign-posted Luogosanto. This burial site is estimated to date back to 3500BC and consists of several rectangular tombs of stone slabs encircled by smaller

slabs. There are five central circles that contained bodies buried in a crouching position. Beside each tomb there are standing stones, some of which have fallen over, and small stone boxes for sacrifices.

Although it makes a useful base, the town of Arzachena itself doesn't merit a long visit; the most interesting thing to see is the natural rock sculpture Roccia Il Fungo (Mushroom Rock) at the end of Via Limbara.

✚ 161 D4

Nuraghe Albucciu
🕐 Jul–Sep daily 9–8; Easter–Jun, Oct 9–1, 3–7 💶 Inexpensive

Coddu Vecchiu
🕐 Jul–Sep daily 9–8; Easter–Jun, Oct 9–1, 3–7 💶 Inexpensive

Tomba dei Giganti di Li Lolghi and Necropoli di Li Muri
☎ 340 8209749 🕐 Easter–Oct daily 9–7; Nov–Easter phone for times 💶 Moderate

Arzachena's Mushroom Rock

Where to … Stay

Prices
Expect to pay per double room, per night
€ under €90 €€ €90–€155 €€€ €155–€250 €€€€ over €250

Hotel Cavour €–€€

This small hotel with 21 rooms is in the centre of Olbia's old town. Tastefully refurbished, it is mostly cool white with pastel shades. There is a pleasant outdoor terrace, where breakfast is served in summer, and on-site parking.

➕ 161 D3 ⊠ Via Cavour 22
☎ 0789 204033; fax: 0789 201096;
www.cavourhotel.it

Hotel Centrale €€

This very central hotel was totally refurbished at the end of 2006. Clean and welcoming, with plenty of marble and minimalist lines, the rooms are pleasant and comfortable. Stays are on a B&B basis only.

➕ 161 D3 ⊠ Corso Umberto 85
☎ 0789 23017; fax: 0789 26464;
email: info@hotel-olbia.it

Hotel Gallura €€

This family-run hotel, near both the train and bus stations, is pleasingly decorated in traditional Sardinian style. The acclaimed restaurant (▶ 133) serves excellent breakfasts.

➕ 161 D3 ⊠ Corso Umberto 145
☎ 0789 24648; fax: 0789 24629

Hotel Abi d'Oru €€€–€€€€

Lying on the Marinella Gulf, 6km (3.5 miles) from Porto Rotondo, this salmon-coloured resort style hotel is located on a beautiful bay. The rooms are comfortable, unclutered and of a good size and most enjoy sea views. In the grounds there is a large freshwater swimming pool, a lake that attracts birdlife and chanting frogs, and paths leading down to the white sandy beach. There are two bars and two restaurants and a pizzeria on the beach. Facilities include a children's club and tennis courts.

➕ 161 E4 ⊠ Golfo di Marinella,
Porto Rotondo ☎ 0789 309019; fax:
0789 32044; www.altamarea.it
🕓 Apr–Oct

Hotel Baja €€€

This hotel was totally refurbished in 2006 and is now a 4-star property 200m (220 yards) from the seafront. Designed by a French architect, the interior is a vision in white and minimalist in style. The 61 rooms are spacious and comfortable, and there's a penthouse suite with an outdoor terrace and Jacuzzi/hot tub. The restaurant is good, the outdoor swimming pool inviting, and the large, fully equipped spa with complete wellness and fitness centre caters to all your health and beauty needs.

➕ 161 D4 ⊠ Via Nazionale,
Cannigione ☎ 0789 892041;
www.hotelbaja.it 🕓 Apr–Sep

Cala di Volpe €€€€

The glitziest of all the Starwood properties, this is a fantasy of Moroccan/troglodyte-inspired architecture originally designed by French architects Michele Busiri and Jacques Couelle. Designed to replicate a fishing village, it has its own private port and jetty jutting out into the eponymous bay. The décor is rustic, with rough plaster walls and older style furniture, but the refurbished bathrooms are decorated with Sardinian marble and handmade ceramics. The clientele is glamorous, rich and famous and the poolside buffets are legendary for their celebrity-spotting opportunities. There is a seawater swimming pool, nine-hole putting green, sauna and fitness centre.

✚ 161 D4 ⊠ Porto Cervo ☎ 0789 976111; www.starwoodhotels.com ⏲ Mar–Oct

Li Capanni €€€

Located between Cannigione and Palau, this oasis of calm is set in 5ha (12 acres) with its own secluded beach. The owner is musician Peter Gabriel, who has overseen the creation of the simple but charming accommodation in six terracotta-coloured cottages. The private terrace restaurant has open views of the sea and the nearby island of La Maddalena, and serves excellent Sardinian cuisine. The small friendly team can organise excursions to the nearby islands, vineyards and archaeological sites.

✚ 161 D4 ⊠ Località Li Capanni, Arzachena ☎ 0789 86041; www.licapanni.com ⏲ May–Sep

Cervo Hotel €€€€

The most "villagey" of all the Starwood hotels, this is right in the heart of Porto Cervo in the piazzetta, with views over the marina. There are two wings – the Tennis Club, which has 16 rooms, and the Cervo Wing, with the more expensive rooms. The rustic rooms have an understated elegance, and most have their own terrace or balcony with views over the harbour, pool or piazzetta. There are five stylish restaurants in and around the hotel, and the exclusive designer boutiques and bars are just a glance away.

✚ 161 D4 ⊠ Piazzetta, Porto Cervo ☎ 0789 93111; www.sheraton.com

Hotel Pitrizza €€€€

Small and über-exclusive, this villa-style hotel is the perfect hideaway for couples. It is also the most expensive of the 5-star hotels on the Costa Smeralda. It is understated yet very sophisticated, with its own private beach and an infinity pool carved out of granite rocks. The décor is traditional Sardinian and all 55 rooms are elegant and, as you would expect at this price, service is impeccable. The Pitrizza Restaurant and Grill next to the pool has splendid views over the sea, and the Pitrizza bar has a spacious terrace.

✚ 161 D4 ⊠ Porto Cervo ☎ 0789 930111; www.starwoodhotels.com ⏲ May–Sep

Hotel Romazzino €€€€

This 5-star luxurious hotel is one of the most desirable and expensive on the island. Set in flower-filled gardens with its own beach, it is built in typical Sardinian style, with curved, whitewashed walls. Inside, the furnishings and colourful tiles are made from natural local materials, and all the well-equipped bedrooms have balconies or terraces. Of the three flagship Starwood hotels on the Costa Smeralda, this is the one best suited to families with its "Toy Club",

incorporating playground, children's dining facilities and babysitting. It has the Romazzino restaurant, Bar Ginepro, barbecue, seawater swimming pool, tennis, water sports and fitness centre.

✚ 161 D4 ⊠ Porto Cervo ☎ 0789 977111; www.starwoodhotels.com/italy ⏲ Apr–Oct

Marinaro €€

This pleasant peach-coloured 3-star hotel is in the centre of the town in a quiet street, but close to the beach. Inside, green and white stripes are the signature colour scheme, and the airy bedrooms have been tastefully refurbished. French windows open on to balconies and there are lovely views from the top floor. There is also a good restaurant. It is family run with charming, helpful staff.

✚ 160 B5 ⊠ Via Angioy 48 ☎ 0789 754112; fax: 0789 755817; www.hotel-marinaro.it

Where to...
Eat and Drink

Prices

Expect to pay for a three-course meal for one, excluding drinks and service
€ under €26 €€ €26–€55 €€€ over €55

ÓLBIA AND ÍSOLA DI TAVOLARA

Da Antonio €

Good fixed-price menus and pizzas are served in this stone-clad trattoria in the centre of Ólbia.
➕ 161 D3 ⊠ Via Garibaldi 48, Ólbia ☎ 0789 609082

Ristorante Gallura €€

This very popular restaurant serves excellent local Gallurese dishes in elegant yet rustic surroundings. The cuisine is a blend of the traditional and creative. Specials include *anemoni di mare fritti* (fried sea urchins), rabbit in saffron and mussels. You must reserve ahead.
➕ 161 D3 ⊠ Corso Umberto 145, Ólbia ☎ 0789 24648 ⓒ Tue–Sun

La Lanterna da Giacomo €–€€

In the heart of Ólbia, this restaurant/pizzeria is in an intimate subterranean setting where the speciality is the bounty of the sea, though there's plenty for vegetarians and carnivores too. Portions are extremely generous and the home-made puddings are especially delectable.
➕ 161 D3 ⊠ Via Ólbia 13, Ólbia ☎ 0789 23082 ⓒ Summer daily; winter Thu–Tue

Ristorante da Tonino €€

Tonino's is run by the present-day "king" of Tavolara. There is an enticing verandah on the beach and the speciality is fish and seafood, served with great aplomb.
➕ 161 D3 ⊠ Via Tavolara 14 ☎ 0789 58570 ⓒ Summer only

COSTA SMERALDA

L'Ancora €€

About 1km (0.5 miles) north of Cannigione, this is a deservedly popular restaurant. Focaccia bread smeared with olive oil and rosemary or pecorino cheese is offered as a complimentary starter. Antipasti include smoked tuna and lobster, the woodburning oven makes delicious fresh pizzas and there's an excellent range of meat dishes.
➕ 161 D4 ⊠ Località La Conta, Cannigione ☎ 0789 86086

Antonella & Gigi Ristorante-Pizzeria €€

This rustic, family-run restaurant is very good value for the location. Expect classic dishes such as *insalata di mare* (seafood salad), *prosciutto e melone* (melon and ham), and mixed grilled fish and a "catch of the day". The food is fresh and simply prepared, and there are traditional murals on the walls.
➕ 161 E4 ⊠ Villaggio Juniperus, Porto Rotondo ☎ 0789 34238 ⓒ Wed–Mon 12–3, 7–11

Mama Latina €€

This pizzeria/restaurant is one of the few to open all year round. Given the exclusive surroundings, dining here is a reasonable option with inexpensive pizzas in the front café and good salads and fish dishes on offer in the stylish dining room.
➕ 161 D4 ⊠ Porto Cervo Marina ☎ 0789 91312 ⓒ Apr–Sep daily; Oct–Mar Mon–Sat

Tanit €€€

This is the place to go if you want to push the boat out, literally, as it overlooks the very exclusive marina. Drinks are served on the panoramic terrace before a gourmet feast of fish and seafood specialities, although Argentine beef also features. Service is very attentive and the price is very high.

🔒 161 D4 ✉ Poltu Quatu (between Báia Sardinia and Porto Cervo)
☎ 0789 955008 🕐 Summer daily bar from 6pm, dinner from 7.30

LA MADDALENA

La Grotta €€

This long-established family restaurant is in an alley off the Via Italia with tables spilling out onto the pavement. Enzo, the proprietor, is an excellent host and the environment is rustic, atmospheric and always bustling. Fish and seafood is piled high in tantalising dishes such as *penne alla grotta* (seafood pasta) or *aragosta sette-otto* – the signature lobster dish.

🔒 161 D5 ✉ Via Principe di Napoli 3, La Maddalena ☎ 0789 737228; www.lagrotta.it 🕐 May–Sep

Where to... Shop

The pretty resorts of Palau, Santa Teresa di Gallura, Báia Sardinia and Cannigione might lack the glamour and exclusivity of Porto Cervo and Porto Rotondo, but many visitors will prefer their laid-back, unpretentious feel. Each has its own smattering of souvenir boutiques and night markets (the best is in Palau and stays open until 1am in the peak season).

On La Maddalena, be sure to visit **Sardegna da Mangiare e da Bere** on Piazza Garibaldi (tel: 0789 73108), a veritable Aladdin's cave of Sardinian specialities. There is everything here, from cheese and salamis to pasta, *dolci sardi* and wines and *mirto liqueur*, all beautifully and oh-so-temptingly displayed.

Where to... Be Entertained

CLASSICAL MUSIC

On the Costa Smeralda, the **Chiesa di Stella Maris** in Porto Cervo has classical music concerts in the summer. Ólbia has an annual summer festival, **L'Estate Olbiense**, from the end of July, with performances and concerts taking place in Piazza Margherita.

NIGHTLIFE

The main action is a couple of kilometres south of Porto Cervo, where the trio of the Costa Smeralda's most happening clubs are on the same road. The **Sopravento** (Località Golfo di Pevero; tel: 0789 94717), **Sottovento** (Località Golfo di Pevero; tel: 0789 92243) and **Billionaire Club** (Località Alto Pevero; tel: 0789 94192) all open only in summer, are very exclusive, very expensive and have very strict door codes. To get in you need to act the part and look seriously moneyed. Plenty of celebs such as Paris Hilton and P Diddy have been spotted in the flickering candlelight and secluded corners of the Moroccan-style Billionaire Club.

For lower-key entertainment and people-watching in Porto Cervo, the **Café du Port** in Porto Vecchio is very popular.

In Ólbia the lively **Planet Café La Moride** in Viale Aldo Moro (tel: 0789 598559) opens its doors onto a terrace in summer.

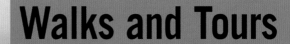

Walks and Tours

1 Cágliari
Walk

DISTANCE 4km (2.5 miles) **TIME** 3–4 hours
START POINT Bastione San Remy ✚ 170 B4 **END POINT** Via Roma ✚ 170 B3

Cágliari's Romanesque cathedral

This walk takes you from the heart of medieval Cágliari at the Bastione San Remy, past the amphitheatre and botanic garden, down to the café-lined Via Roma.

1–2
Start your walk from **Bastione San Remy** on Piazza Costituzione. Heading north from the Bastione, walk up the Via Fossario to Piazza Palazzo, the heart of the Castello district, and you will come to the **Cattedrale** on your right. Look at the Pisan Romanesque façade and then go inside to see the baroque/Gothic decorations (▶ 46). The next building on your left, on the northeastern side of the Piazza Palazzo, is the **Palazzo Viceregio**, its pale green neoclassical façade contrasting with the deep rust shutters (Tue–Fri 8:30–2, 3–7, Sat 8:30–2). The reception rooms are adorned with Murano glass chandeliers, frescoed ceilings and silk-lined walls – and portraits of the Piedmontese viceroys who formerly governed Sardinia from here.

2–3
Continue northwards and turn right into the little Piazzetta Mercede Mundula. From here there are glorious views over the bay and convenient benches from which to admire them. Continue up the Via Pietro Martini to the Piazza Indipendenza. At the head of this piazza is the **Torre di San Pancrazio** (Tue–Sun 9–1, 3:30–7:30). Similar to the Torre dell' Elefante (▶ 46), this is one of the city's medieval constructions not to have undergone "ruinous modification", as the plaque tells you. It was built by the Pisans in 1305 and is 55m (180 feet) high; from the top there are spectacular views. Proceed through the archway to the sloping Piazza Arsenale to arrive at the **Cittadella dei Musei**.

3–4
There are four museums here – the Pinacoteca (art gallery); the Mostra di Cere Anatomiche, a waxworks of rather gory anatomic sections; the Museo d'Arte Siamese

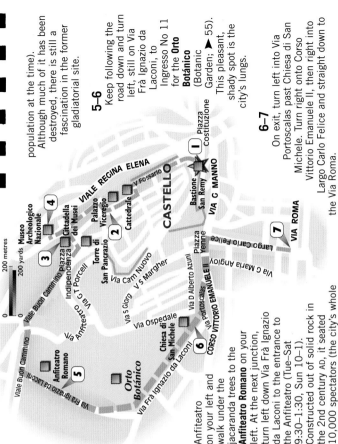

population at the time). Although much of it has been destroyed, there is still a fascination in the former gladiatorial site.

5–6

Keep following the road down and turn left, still on Via Frà Ignazio da Laconi, to Ingresso No 11 for the **Orto Botánico** (Botanic Garden; ➤ 55). This pleasant, shady spot is the city's lungs.

6–7

On exit, turn left into Via Portoscalas past Chiesa di San Michele. Turn right onto Corso Vittorio Emanuele II, then right into Largo Carlo Felice and straight down to the Via Roma.

Remains of the Roman amphitheatre

(Southeast Asian art); and the highlight, the Museo Archeológico (➤ 47).

4–5

After leaving the museum, turn right and go out of Porta Cristina (signposted "*ingresso al castello*"). Turn right along Viale Buon Cammino, then cross over the road with Via

Anfiteatro on your left and walk under the jacaranda trees to the **Anfiteatro Romano** on your left. At the next junction, turn left down Via Frà Ignazio da Laconi to the entrance to the Anfiteatro (Tue–Sat 9:30–1:30, Sun 10–1). Constructed out of solid rock in the 2nd century AD, it seated 10,000 spectators (the city's whole

Taking a Break

Il Caffè at no 76 Largo Carlo Felice is a good place for a drink and a browse in their very good bookshop.

2 Cágliari to Villasímius

Drive

This drive takes you past the Golfo degli Ángeli (Bay of Angels) along the Strada Panorámica, which overlooks lovely beaches backed by low hills and covered with Mediterranean *macchia*. As you leave Cágliari behind, the coast becomes much quieter, the road twists and turns over hilly terrain with dramatic views of the sea, white sands and delightfully secluded coves begging to be explored.

DISTANCE 51km (32 miles) to Villasímius (but with detours to beaches)
TIME 2–3 hours or a day with all detours
START POINT Cágliari Airport ✚ 168 A2   **END POINT** Villasímius ✚ 169 D1

Rocky shoreline between Cágliari and Villasímius

1–2

Start from **Cágliari airport** (6km/3.5 miles northwest of Cágliari centre) and going south-east take the SS554, following the signs for Quartu S Elena and Villasímius. This is mainly dual carriageway around the ring road (and no tolls payable). As you get close to the sea, look out for flamingos in the lagoons left and right, Stagno Simbrizzi and Stagno di Quartu respectively. To reach Poetto beach from here, turn west on the coast road past Spiaggia di Quartu and on to Marina Piccola on **Poetto** beach.

1–2 (alternative)

If you're travelling from the centre of Cágliari, go southeast on Via Roma towards Largo Carlo Felice, continue on the road which becomes Viale Armando Diaz, then on to Ponto Vittorio and slightly left at Viale Poetto, then left at Via Lungo Saline. Stop at vast **Poetto** beach (more than 5km/3 miles long) with its fine, white sand, and admire the

Boats in the harbour at Villasímius

Taking a Break

Stop for lunch at **Ristorante da Barbara**, Strada Provinciale per Villasimíus, in Solánas, tel: 070 750630, or have a drink overlooking the marina at **Café del Porto** (➤ 60) in Porto di Villasimíus.

is the most southeasterly point of Sardinia and from here there are excellent views. Rejoin the main road, which brings you into Villasimíus.

lagoon of Molentargius behind it, which is frequented by flamingos and many other wetland birds.

and a lovely panorama.

4–5

On the coastal road follow the signs for

2–3

Continue along the panoramic Cágliari–Villasimíus coastal road to the locality of **Sant'Andrea** (on the left). For the beach turn right a little further along into Via Taormina, which brings you to the shore. On the western side there are remains of a 3rd century AD Roman villa and thermal baths.

3–4

Return to the scenic coast road and after just over 13km (8 miles) you arrive at **Geremeás** with its long, white sandy beaches. Nearby, to the east, is **Torre delle Stelle** where you can take a dirt road east from the centre of the village to the beach. There are bars and shops by the white-golden sand

Solánas, about 32km (20 miles) from Cágliari. The main road loops around, giving access to the beach at the main car park in the centre, but choose the prettier, eastern side, remarkable for its dune at the base of **Capo Boi**. The large, golden sandy beach extends to the west of this promontory, overseen by a 16th-century watchtower, Torre di Capo Boi.

5–6

Continue back on the main road and after 11km (7 miles) take the road to the right going south signposted **Capo Carbonara**. This

3 Oristano and Sínis Peninsula

Drive

DISTANCE 49km (30 miles) **TIME** Half a day
START/END POINT Oristano ✚ 162 C3

This leisurely drive takes you to the seaside resort of Marina di Torre Grande and then through the "flamingo heaven" lagoon world of Mistras and Cábras before reaching the tip of the Sínis Peninsula at the remains of the gloriously sited ancient city of Thárros.

1–2

Take the SS292 north from Oristano towards Marina di Torre Grande and Cúglieri. A long bridge crosses the Tirso, after which you come to a fork in the road. Take the left fork, following the signs for Cábras/Thárros and keep following signs for San Giovanni di Sínis. About 9km (5.5 miles) outside Oristano you come to **Marina di Torre Grande** (▶ 71). This is a buzzing seaside resort (in season) with a long, white sandy beach that shelves gently and has plenty of watersports facilities.

2–3

Head back to the main road and at the inter-

Volleyball on the beach at Marina di Torre Grande

section take the left-hand turn towards San Giovanni di Sínis. On both sides you now have lagoons. On your left is the Stagno di Mistras, while on the right is the **Stagno di Cábras** – the largest in Italy at 2,000ha (5,000 acres). Besides flamingos, the lagoon also teems with fish, especially mullet, which

is used to make the prized *bottarga* (mullet roe). Go straight on past a right turn towards Thárros to **San Giovanni di Sínis**.

3–4

This sleepy fishing village's Chiesa di San Giovanni di Sínis is, after Cagliari's San Saturnino, the oldest church in Sardinia, dating from AD476. The interior is refreshingly bare and simple. Behind the church, near the sea, are some remaining thatched *domus de cruccuri* (rush huts) once used by fishermen. Leaving the church on your left continue down the road to **Thárros.**

4–5

Founded around 730BC, **Thárros** (▶ 69) was the most prosperous of the west coast Phoenician port cities. After the Roman conquest in 238BC, however, it gradually fell into disuse as trade shifted to Oristano in 1070. The archaeological site reveals mostly the Roman city, but there is still a temple with Doric half-columns and a children's

Taking a Break

Have a drink in Marina di Torre Grande on the palm-lined esplanade, or in San Salvatore in the "wild west saloon", the only bar in the hamlet.

5–6

Return the same way until you reach the left turn to San Salvatore/Riola, 4km (2.5 miles) north. Once the setting for spaghetti westerns, the dusty little town of **San Salvatore** (▶ 75) is hugely atmospheric – although often deserted except for the Barefoot Race in September.

6–7

Go northeast on SP7 towards SP59 for 7km (4.5 miles) then turn right at the SS292 after 1km (0.5 miles) and take the next right at Via Sant'Anna into Riola Sardo. Continue on the SS292 back to Oristano.

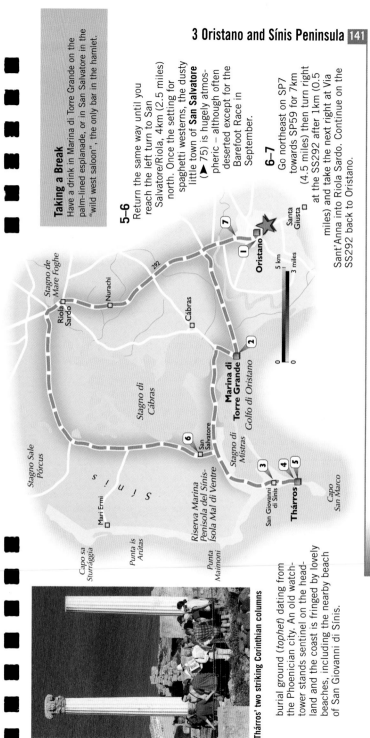

Thárros' two striking Corinthian columns

burial ground (*tophet*) dating from the Phoenician city. An old watchtower stands sentinel on the headland and the coast is fringed by lovely beaches, including the nearby beach of San Giovanni di Sínis.

4 Alghero
Walk

This walk takes you through the old town of Alghero, protected by ancient walls and towers. In the web of narrow streets you will pass washing hung out like

Statues inside San Francesco church

DISTANCE 2km (1.2 miles) **TIME** 2–3 hours
START POINT Piazza Porta Terra ✚ 170 D1 **END POINT** Piazza Civica ✚ 170 B2

bunting beneath the shuttered windows and the city's most important churches and museums. The walk culminates in the main piazza, where Charles V addressed the crowds in 1541 before going off to fight the Turks.

1–2
Start at **Piazza Porta Terra** opposite the top end of the Giardino Pùbblico. The Porta Terra was one of the walled town's two gates, and is now an interpretation centre; climb the 32 steps to the top for excellent views of the town. Coming out of here, turn left into Carrer de los Arjoles and then right into Via Ambrogion Machin. At the end of this road turn right into Via Carlo Alberto and you'll come to the **Chiesa di San Francesco** on the right. This is one of Alghero's landmarks, with its stately, pointed Aragonese tower, and is an excellent example of Catalan architecture. Parts of the honey-coloured cloisters date back to the 13th century. Concerts are staged in this lovely setting during the summer.

2–3
From the church turn left and walk back down **Via Carlo Alberto**. This street is Alghero's main shopping hub, full of boutiques and jewellery shops brimming with coral. Continue straight on crossing over Via Gilbert Ferret. Known as the *"quatre contonades"* (four sides), this junction was where piecemeal labourers would assemble in the hope of getting work over the centuries. After this, on the left-hand side, you come to the 17th-century **Chiesa di San Michele**. This opulent baroque church dominates the skyline with its glistening ceramic dome and has fine altar paintings inside.

3–4
From San Michele walk back to Via Gilbert Ferret and turn left, then right into Via Principe Umberto, one of the old centre's most attractive lanes. The 17th-century **Palazzo Machin** (Nos 9–11) was built for a local bishop and, although now crumbling, still has fine Catalan-Gothic windows.

The map shows:
VIA CAGLIARI
VIA SASSARI
VIA SASSARI
Piazza Porta Terra
Torre di Porta a Terra ★
Via Roma
Giardino Pubblico
i 1
Piazza Civica
Palazzo d'Albis 5
Porta a Mare 5
Piazza Duomo
Museo Diocesano d'Arte Sacra 4
Cattedrale 4
Porto
via
Via Principe Umberto
Palazzo Machin
Via Arduino
Via Mallorca
Via Carlo Alberto Roma
Piazza Municipio
Chiesa di San Francesco 2
Via A Machin
Ferret
Gilbert
Via
Piazza Ginnasio
Chiesa di San Michele 3
0 100 metres
0 100 yards

The cathedral's neoclassical façade

Continue up the street and ahead of you, just to the right, is the cathedral's octagonal campanile. Walk around into Piazza Duomo and see the **Cattedrale di Santa Maria**. Inside there is a jumble of styles and overblown baroque touches although some parts of the original 16th-century building remain.

4–5

Go out of the Cattedrale and head next door to the **Museo Diocesano d'Arte Sacra**, housed in the former Rosario church. This is the perfect setting for an array of priceless religious art. Walk east past Via Maiorca, Via Carlo Alberto and Vicolo Sena till you arrive at **Piazza Civica**, the old town's main square, known as "*Il Salotto*" (the dining room). It is just inside the Port a Mare (Sea Gate) and is full of outdoor bars and parasols. On the opposite side of the piazza is the Gothic Palazzo d'Albis, from where Charles V told the assembled throng, "*Estade todos caballeros*" ("you are all knights").

Taking a Break

Rather like a pub, the **Jamaica Inn** at Via Principe Umberto 57 (Tue–Sun) is a good place for a snack and a drink – more wines than beers. **Il Ghiotto** (▶ 114), Piazza Civica 23, is a great place for lunch as it's a wine bar and a delicatessen.

5 Gennargentu Mountains

Drive

This scenic drive takes you through granite-strewn rolling countryside framed by lush vegetation of Mediterranean *macchia*, cork, holm and oak trees. There are tracks and gorges and majestic mountains, and vineyards around Oliena that produce some of the island's finest wines.

DISTANCE 77km (48 miles) **TIME** Half-day to full day
START/END POINT Núoro ✚ 164 C4

The road from Núoro to Monte Ortobene

1–2

Leave Núoro heading east on the Via Trieste. Continue on this road, which becomes the Via Ballero, then turn left at Viale La Solitudine. After 0.3km (330 yards) bear slightly right onto the SP42, Via Monte Ortobene. Continue along this panoramic road as it twists upwards. (From Núoro the journey is about 8km/5 miles.) You will come to some speed humps on the road followed by souvenir stalls and a couple of bars/restaurants. Leave your car in the car park near the top of **Monte Ortobene** and follow the faded yellow sign saying

"Il Redentore". A walk of around 100m (110 yards) along a dusty track brings you to 49 rock steps up to the bronze sculpture of Christ the Redeemer (➤ 92).

2–3

The next stage, **Oliena**, is 12km (7.5 miles) away. Leave Monte Ortobene heading north-west on the SP42 towards the SP45/Via Valverde. Bear slightly left at SP45/Viale La Solitudine and turn left at SP45. Take a sharp left at the SS129. After 4.3km (2.7 miles) turn right at the SP22 and continue on the SP22 by turning left. Bear slightly right at Via Raffaele Calamida then turn right at Via Núoro/SP46 and follow tourist information signs to the main Via Deledda. Here is a good place to pick up information on the area and excursions (including Tiscali and Gola Su Gorruppu). Oliena is a very pretty town full of white-washed old houses with balconies, terraces and strange little chimneypots. It was also the haunt of bandits until fairly recent times

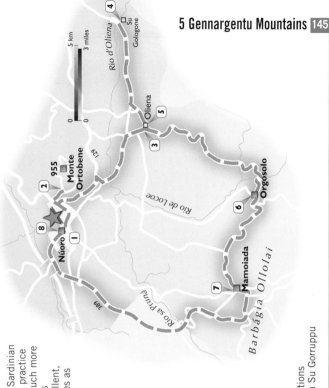

and many of the old Sardinian customs are put into practice here. It also has a much more savoury reputation as producer of the excellent, fruity Cannonau wines as well as for beautiful filigree silver and gold jewellery and delicately embroidered silk shawls.

3–4

A little diversion 6km (3.5 miles) east on the Dorgali road/SP46 takes you to **Su Gologone**, named after its spring, which rises close to the church of San Giovanni. It is also a good spot for embarking on expeditions to Tiscali and/or Gola Su Gorruppu

A mountain cow – a common sight in the Gennargentu

but note that these would take up around four hours and involve some arduous trekking (▶ 90–91, 92). There's also a luxurious hotel, the Su Gologone, which offers many expeditions and has a good restaurant.

4–5
Retrace your steps on the SP46 to Oliena.

5–6
After about 7km (4.5 miles) outside Oliena turn left at the SP58 and follow this twisting, scenic road for about 11km (7 miles) until you see the entrance to **Orgosolo** (▶ 94). Known as the "capital of the Barbàgia" and former refuge of the area's most notorious bandits, it is also famous for the murals that cover every available space depicting political themes and the locals' struggle to maintain their culture.

6–7
From Orgosolo head west for 10km (6 miles) to **Mamoiada** (▶ 93). Take the SP22/Corso Repùblica towards Via di Vittorio and continue on the SP22. Famous for its masked festivals, especially at Carnival time in February/March, Mamoiada has the interesting Museo delle Maschere

Mediterranee showing the *mamuthones* costumed figures for which the town is famous.

7–8
From Mamoiada head southwest on Via Matteotti towards Via Núoro and turn right, then bear slightly right again at SS389/Via Vittorio Emanuele II and follow the SS389 to Núoro.

Taking a Break
Under shady eucalyptus trees in Su Gologone is a good place to enjoy a picnic, with free-flowing therapeutic spring water. Or treat yourself to a delicious meal at the Su Gologone restaurant/hotel (▶ 97).

One of Orgosolo's striking murals

Pottery for sale in Orgoloso

6 Ísola Caprera
Walk

This walk takes you through the archipelago's greenest island, known also as "Garibaldi's island". He loved Caprera's freedom and peace so much that he chose to spend the last years of his life here (▶128). Stroll through *macchia* and past green pines enjoying stunning views over the surrounding islands and across to Corsica. The island's highest peak, pink granite Monte Telaione, reaches up to 212m (695 feet), where you may see peregrine falcons. You could also choose to take a detour to the lovely Cala Coticcio beach.

1–2

From the car park, take the footpath that forks right into the *macchia* going south. Follow this main path through the scented myrtle, juniper, lentisk, lavender and wild flowers, ignoring the short tracks down to the coast. After about 15 minutes you come to a grove of umbrella pine trees. Turn right at the

DISTANCE 12.5km (8 miles) **TIME** 4 hours
START/END POINT Car park, Caprera (350m/380 yards after the causeway from La Maddalena)
🔳 161 D5

next fork and on your right is the Cala Stagnali – a little cove with coarse sand. Keep straight on the main track to an asphalt road onto which you bear right. At the fork turn left and begin the ascent looking out over the archipelago's islands and Corsica. After about an hour and a quarter of walking, you'll see the peak of **Poggio Rasu** (Bare Hill) on your right. The road bends to the left but carry straight along the track to the World War II gun emplacement built from granite.

2–3

Return to the bend and continue right, ascending along the road. After a short distance the road begins to level out and descend. At a T-junction turn right past a derelict fountain on the left and a concrete building on the right. Continue along this road to a lay-by on the left, then after 50m (55 yards) take a little detour by turning sharp right and climb up the steps to **Monte Teliaone** – Caprera's highest peak – with its

The views from Ísola Caprera are idyllic

lookout tower. From here you could take a detour down a steep path to the right followed by a flight of rocky steps made by the army to the little **Cala Coticcio** beach. Note that it is a very steep incline.

3–4

Return to the road and turn right to continue. After about 2 hours and 45 minutes (in total), shortly after you pass a derelict house on the left, follow the road as it bears left and the asphalted road runs out. On reaching a track junction, turn down to the left. (The track straight ahead leads to Monte Arbuticci's gun emplacement.) Ignore the two turns on your right and go straight ahead.

4–5

At a junction go left past two Military Zone buildings on the right and up to a reservoir (about 3 hours and 15 minutes). Cross the wall of the dam, following the ascending

path, which eventually flattens out leading to a car park. Follow the granite drive on the right past wind-sculpted granite rocks to the **Casa Garibaldi**.

5–6

Before the Garibaldi buildings, take the short concrete drive on the left to a little terrace. Carry on downhill on the path below the enclosed estate until the path descends between rocks. At a small house bear right before joining a road which takes you past houses. Follow the main road left back to the small car park.

A blissfully quiet road on Ísola Caprera.

Taking a Break

Take a picnic and plenty of water to enjoy the peace of this lovely, wild island. Try to avoid weekends as locals like to drive on these tracks then.

Practicalities

Websites
www.regione.sardegna.it
www.sardinia.net
www.sarnow.com

In Italy
Italian State Tourist Board
Via Marghera 2/6
00185 Rome
☎ 06 49711
www.enit.it

In the UK
ENIT
1 Princes Street
London W1B 2AY
☎ 020 7408 1254
www.enit.it

BEFORE YOU GO

WHAT YOU NEED

	● Required ○ Suggested ▲ Not required △ Not applicable	Some countries require a passport to remain valid for a minimum period (usually at least 6 months) beyond the date of entry – check before you travel.	UK	Germany	USA	Canada	Australia	Ireland	Netherlands	Spain
Passport			●	●	●	●	●	●	●	●
Visa (for less than 3 months)			▲	▲	▲	▲	▲	▲	▲	▲
Onward or return ticket			○	○	●	●	●	○	○	○
Health inoculations (tetanus and polio)			▲	▲	▲	▲	▲	▲	▲	▲
Registration document/insurance certificate (if own car)			●	●	●	●	●	●	●	●
Travel insurance			○	○	○	○	○	○	○	○
Driver's licence (national)			●	●	●	●	●	●	●	●

WHEN TO GO

Cágliari

High season   Low season

JAN	FEB	MAR	APR	MAY	JUN	JUL	AUG	SEP	OCT	NOV	DEC
10°C	11°C	13°C	19°C	22°C	25°C	31°C	31°C	26°C	22°C	16°C	12°C
50°F	52°F	55°F	66°F	72°F	77°F	88°F	88°F	79°F	72°F	61°F	53°F

☀ Sun   Very Wet   Wet   Sun/Showers

Sardinia has a very **pleasant six-month summer**, usually hot and dry from May to October but cooled by a breeze as it is the middle of the Mediterranean. In March and April evenings can be cool, but this is a **good time for walking**, the island is covered in flowers, and there are also a number of excellent festivals. From May onwards it is usually warm enough for swimming. July and August are the **peak season** and are often swelteringly hot as well as extremely busy. September can also be very hot, but it is much less crowded. Autumn sees a second flowering of plants, while in the winter the weather can still be warm and clear – but there are **snowfalls** in the interior, where it is possible to ski. Note that many hotels around the coast are only open from May to September.

GETTING THERE

By Air Sardinia is served by three airports: Alghero in the northwest, Ólbia in the northeast and Cágliari in the south.

From the UK From London airports, easyJet flies to Cágliari and Ólbia, and Ryanair flies to Alghero. Other scheduled airlines operate in the summer such as BMI and British Airways, and there are many regional flights too. The flight time is 2–3 hours.

From the US and Canada There are no direct flights to the island, but there are flights to the mainland from several cities. The main hubs are Milan and Rome, from where there are plenty of connecting flights. The national airline, Alitalia, has the widest selection of routes between the US and Italy. Flying time to the mainland is 8–10 hours from the east coast and around 11 hours from the west coast. Connections to Sardinia take another hour or two. The most frequent flights are between Rome and Cágliari.

From Australia and New Zealand There are no direct flights but Air New Zealand and Qantas fly to Milan and Rome, from where it is easy to pick up a connecting flight. You could also fly to the UK first and then pick up a flight as there are so many options. Flying time to mainland Italy from Australia's east coast is 21 hours and from New Zealand is 24 hours.

By Sea There are several options to cross the English Channel to France and many routes from France and Italy to Sardinia: Marseille to Porto Tórres (northwest coast), Rome (Civitavecchia) to Golfo Aranci or Ólbia (northeast coast) and Genova to Porto Tórres or Ólbia, for example. There are also fast ferries from Nice to Bastia in Corsica and daily ferries from Bonifacio to Santa Teresa on the northern tip of Sardinia.

TIME

 Like mainland Italy, Sardinia is one hour ahead of GMT, although daylight saving applies from April to October, making it GMT +2.

CURRENCY AND FOREIGN EXCHANGE

Currency The legal currency of Sardinia is the euro (€), which is split into 100 cents (*centésimi*). Euro notes are issued in denominations of 5, 10, 20, 50, 100, 200 and 500. There are eight different coin denominations – 1 and 2 euros, then 50, 20, 10, 5, 2 and 1 cents. All euro coins and notes are accepted in all EU member states.

Exchange Cash and most major traveller's cheques can be exchanged at banks and at kiosks (*cambio*) at the airports and large hotels.

Credit and debit cards Credit cards are widely accepted, except in B&Bs and *agriturismi*, but many smaller establishments prefer cash. Most towns have a bank with an ATM from which you can withdraw cash with credit or debit card, although using the former is usually expensive.

TIME DIFFERENCES

GMT
12 noon

Sardinia
1pm

Netherlands
1pm

USA (West Coast)
4am

USA (New York) 7am

Australia
(Sydney) 10pm

WHEN YOU ARE THERE

CLOTHING SIZES

UK	Rest of Europe	USA/Canada		
36	46	36		
38	48	38		
40	50	40		Suits
42	52	42		
44	54	44		
46	56	46		
7	41	8		
7.5	42	8.5		
8.5	43	9.5		Shoes
9.5	44	10.5		
10.5	45	11.5		
11	46	12		
14.5	37	14.5		
15	38	15		
15.5	39/40	15.5		Shirts
16	41	16		
16.5	42	16.5		
17	43	17		
8	34	6		
10	36	8		
12	38	10		Dresses
14	40	12		
16	42	14		
18	44	16		
4.5	38	6		
5	38	6.5		
5.5	39	7		Shoes
6	39	7.5		
6.5	40	8		
7	41	8.5		

NATIONAL HOLIDAYS

1 Jan	New Year's Day
6 Jan	Epiphany
Mar/Apr	Good Friday and Easter Monday
25 Apr	Liberation Day
1 May	Labour Day
2 Jun	Republic Day
15 Aug	Ferragosto (Assumption)
1 Nov	Ognissanti (All Saints)
8 Dec	Immaculate Conception
25 Dec	Christmas Day
26 Dec	St Stephen's Day

OPENING HOURS

○ Shops   ● Post Offices
● Offices   ● Museums/Monuments
● Banks   ● Pharmacies

8am 9am 10am noon 1pm 2pm 4pm 5pm 7pm

☐ Day   ▨ Midday   ☐ Evening

Shops Shops are usually open Mon–Sat 8–1, 4–7 or 8. Some are closed Monday mornings and all shops, except the odd food shop, are closed on Sundays. Big department stores (only found in Cágliari and Sássari) have continuous opening Mon–Sat 9–8:30.

Museums Times vary but are usually daily 9–1, 4–8 (3–7 in winter). Some museums are closed on Mondays, though some of these will open daily in high season. Archaeological sites are usually open from 9 to one hour before sunset. Many smaller museums and places of interest have very reduced opening hours during winter and some close down completely.

Post offices Post offices are open all day Mon–Fri but only in the morning on Saturdays, until about 1.

Churches Usually open 7 or 8–noon, 4–7. Smaller ones only open for morning and evening services.

EMERGENCY NUMBERS

POLICE 112

FIRE 115 (or 113)

AMBULANCE 118 (or 113)

GENERAL EMERGENCY 113

PERSONAL SAFETY

You're very unlikely to come across any bandits and Sardinia is one of Italy's safest regions. However, in larger cities such as Cágliari it makes sense to take the usual precautions – petty theft related to drug addiction is on the increase.

To be safe:

• Close bags and wear them in front, slung across your body.

• Leave valuables and jewellery in the hotel safe.

• Never leave luggage or other possessions in parked cars.

• Wear your camera and don't leave it unattended in cafés and restaurants.

• Avoid parks late at night.

Police assistance:
☎ **112** from any phone

TELEPHONES

€10 denominations and available from newsstands or *tabacchi*. Tear the perforated corner off before use. Phone tariffs are very expensive – among the highest in Europe. To get through to an English-speaking operator dial 170. The mobile is an indispensable part of Sardinian life. They work on the GSM European standard.

Telecom Italia (TI) payphones can be found on streets and in bars and some restaurants. Usually you need a phonecard (*scheda telefónica*), available in €3, €5 or

International Dialling Codes
Dial 00 followed by

UK:	44
USA / Canada:	1
Irish Republic:	353
Australia:	61
Germany:	49

POST

The postal service is very slow. You can buy stamps (*francobolli*) at post offices, tobacconists (*tabacchi*) and some souvenir shops. Post offices are normally open Mon–Fri 8:10–6:50, Sat 8–1:15.

ELECTRICITY

The current is 220 volts AC. However, appliances requiring 240 volts AC also work. Plugs are standard two-round-pin continental types. UK, North American and Australasian visitors will need an adaptor, and US visitors will need a voltage transformer.

TIPS/GRATUITIES

Small tips are often expected. As a general guide:

Restaurants (service included)	Change
Restaurants (service not included)	10%
Cafés/bars (if service not included)	Change or 10%
Taxis	Discretionary
Tour guides	Discretionary
Porters	€1–€2
Chambermaids	Discretionary
Hairdressers	10%
Toilets	Discretionary

CONSULATES and EMBASSIES

UK
☎ (070) 828628
(Cágliari)

USA
☎ (06) 46741
(Rome)

Ireland
☎ (06) 697 9121
(Rome)

Australia
☎ (06) 8527
2293 (Rome)

Canada
☎ (06) 445981
(Rome)

HEALTH

Insurance You should always take out full travel insurance cover when visiting Sardinia. EU citizens can reclaim medical expenses if they travel with their European Health Insurance Card (EHIC). There are reciprocal arrangements between the Australian Medicare system and Italy, but comprehensive insurance is still advised.

Doctors and Dentists Ask at a pharmacy or your hotel for details of English-speaking doctors. Common ailments include dehydration, sunburn, stomach upsets and mosquito bites. Use insect repellent and sun protection. Dental treatment is not covered by the health service and can be expensive – another reason to carry medical insurance.

Weather The sun is at its hottest in July and August, with temperatures frequently over 30°C (86°F), but it's always possible to cool off in the sea or mountains. Two summer winds sweep across the island – the *maestrale* (mistral) from the northwest, and the sultry, sand-bearing scirocco from the south. You should take a sun hat, high-factor suncream and plenty of water to drink.

Drugs Prescriptions and other medicines are available from pharmacies (*farmacie*), indicated by a large green cross.

Safe Water Tap water is generally safe to drink and is free in bars, although many people choose bottled water. Sardinia has many mountain springs from which you can drink. "*Acqua non potabile*" indicates non-drinking water.

CONCESSIONS

Students/Youths An International Student Identity Card (ISIC) entitles holders to discounts (usually half the normal fee) at museums and archaeological sites. There are three *ostelli per la gioventù* (youth hostels) on the island, which offer inexpensive accommodation; see www.ostellionline.org

Senior Citizens Admission to some sites is reduced for those aged 65 (sometimes 60) or over.

TRAVELLING WITH A DISABILITY

The national museums in Cágliari have dedicated ramps, lifts and lavatories, but otherwise wheelchair access is extremely limited. Prehistoric sites and monuments generally have very difficult access, and the same is true of medieval city centres, which often have cobbled streets. Hotels at the more luxurious end are generally well equipped.

CHILDREN

Children are welcomed with open arms in Sardinia. Many of the resorts have crèches and children's clubs. The sun can be fierce so it is essential to provide little ones with adequate protection against sunburn and dehydration.

TOILETS

There are very few public toilets on the island. Most bars have them (*bagno, gabinetto* or *toilette*) and most are relatively clean, although it's always a good idea to carry some toilet tissue with you.

CUSTOMS

The import of wildlife souvenirs from rare or endangered species may be illegal or require a special permit. Before buying, check your home country's regulations.

USEFUL WORDS AND PHRASES

The official language of Sardinia is Italian, and most Sardinians speak it clearly. The Sardinian language is a melting pot of many influences – around Alghero you will hear Catalan, for example – but if there is one language from which *sardo* takes its root it is Latin, and it is closer to this mother tongue than mainland Italian is; for example Sard for house is *domus* rather than Italian *casa*. The other major difference is the replacement of the Italian definite articles *il*, *la*, *i* and *le* with *su*, *sa*, *sus*, *sos* and *sas*, similar to Catalan. People appreciate your greeting them with a *buon giorno* or *buona sera*. *Grazie* (thank you) should be acknowledged with *prego* (you're welcome). *Permesso*? (May I?) is the polite way of making your way through a crowded street.

SURVIVAL PHRASES

Yes/no **Sì/non**
Please **Per favore**
Thank you **Grazie**
You're welcome **Di niente/prego**
I'm sorry **Mi dispiace**
Goodbye **Arrivederci**
Good morning **Buongiorno**
Goodnight **Buona sera**
How are you? **Come sta?**
How much? **Quanto costa?**
I would like... **Vorrei...**
Open **Aperto**
Closed **Chiuso**
Today **Oggi**
Tomorrow **Domani**
Monday **lunedì**
Tuesday **martedì**
Wednesday **mercoledì**
Thursday **giovedì**
Friday **venerdì**
Saturday **sabato**
Sunday **domenica**

DIRECTIONS

I'm lost **Mi sono perso/a**
Where is...? **Dove si trova...?**
  the station **la stazione**
  the telephone **il telefono**
  the bank **la banca**
  the toilet **il bagno**
Turn left **Volti a sinistra**
Turn right **Volti a destra**
Go straight on **Vada dritto**
At the corner **All'angolo**
  the street **la strada**
  the building **il palazzo**
  the traffic light **il semaforo**
  the crossroads **l'incrocio**
  the signs for...
    le indicazione per...

IF YOU NEED HELP

Help! **Aiuto!**
Could you help me, please?
  Mi potrebbe aiutare?
Do you speak English? **Parla inglese?**
I don't understand **Non capisco**
Please could you call a doctor
  quickly? **Mi chiami presto un
  medico, per favore**

RESTAURANT

I'd like to book a table
  Vorrei prenotare un tavolo
A table for two, please
  Un tavolo per due, per favore
Could we see the menu, please?
  Ci porta la lista, per favore?
What's this? **Cosa è questo?**
A bottle of/a glass of...
  Un bottiglia di/un bicchiere di...
Could I have the bill?
  Ci porta il conto

ACCOMMODATION

Do you have a single/double room?
  Ha una camera singola/doppia?
with/without bath/toilet/shower
  **con/senza vasca/gabinetto/
  doccia**
Does that include breakfast?
  E'inclusa la prima colazione?
Does that include dinner?
  E'inclusa la cena?
Do you have room service?
  C'è il servizio in camera?
Could I see the room?
  E' possibile vedere la camera?
I'll take this room **Prendo questa**
Thanks for your hospitality
  Grazie per l'ospitalità

MENU READER

Sardinian specialities:

cavallo horse
cordula lamb tripe
granelle calf's testicles
porceddu roast suckling pig
sebada doughnut-style confection filled with sweet cheese and honey
suspiros sweets made with almonds, eggs and lemon
zimino russo roasted offal
zurrette black pudding made with sheep's blood

Other menu items:

acciuga anchovy
acqua water
affettati sliced cured meats
affumicato smoked
aglio garlic
agnello lamb
anatra duck
antipasti hors d'oeuvres
arista roast pork
arrosto roast
asparagi asparagus
birra beer
bistecca steak
bollito boiled meat
braciola minute steak
brasato braised
brodo broth
budino pudding
burro butter
cacciagione game
cacciatore, alla rich tomato sauce with mushrooms
caffè corretto/ macchiato coffee with liqueur/spirit, or with a drop of milk
caffè freddo iced coffee
caffè latte milky coffee
caffè lungo weak coffee
caffè ristretto strong coffee
calamaro squid
cappero caper
carciofo artichoke
carne meat
carota carrot
carpa carp
casalingo home-made
cavolfiore cauliflower
cavolo cabbage
ceci chickpeas
cervello brains
cervo venison
cetriolino gherkin
cetriolo cucumber
cicoria chicory
cinghiale boar
cioccolata chocolate
cipolla onion
coda di bue oxtail
coniglio rabbit
contorni vegetables
coperto cover charge
coscia leg of meat
cotolette cutlets
cozze mussels
crema custard
crudo raw
dolci cakes/desserts
erbe aromatiche herbs
facito stuffed
fagioli beans

fagiolini green beans
fegato liver
finocchio fennel
formaggio cheese
forno, al baked
frittata omelette
fritto fried
frizzante fizzy
frulatto whisked
frutta fruit
frutti di mare seafood
funghi mushrooms
gamberetto shrimp
gelato icecream
ghiaccio ice
gnocchi potato dumplings
granchio crab
gran(o)turco corn
griglia, alla grilled
imbottito stuffed
insalata salad
IVA VAT
latte milk
lepre hare
lumache snails
manzo beef
merluzzo cod
miele honey
minestra soup
molluschi shellfish
olio oil
oliva olive
ostrica oyster
pancetta bacon
pane bread
panino roll
panna cream
pastasciutta dried pasta with sauce
pasta sfoglia puff pastry
patate fritte chips
pecora mutton
pecorino sheep's milk cheese
peperoncino chilli
peperone red/ green pepper
pesce fish

petto breast
piccione pigeon
piselli peas
pollame fowl
pollo chicken
polpetta meatball
porto port wine
prezzemolo parsley
primo piatto first course
ragù meat sauce
ripieno stuffed
riso rice
salsiccia sausage
saltimbocca veal with prosciutto and sage
secco dry
secondo piatto main course
senape mustard
servizio compreso service included
sogliola sole
succa di frutta fruit juice
sugo sauce
tonno tuna
uovo affrogato/ in carnica poached egg
uovo al tegamo/ fritto fried egg
uovo alla coque soft boiled egg
uovo alla sodo hard boiled egg
uova strapazzate scambled egg
verdure vegetables
vino bianco white wine
vino rosato rosé wine
vino rosso red wine
vitello veal
zucchero sugar
zucchino courgette
zuppa soup

Atlas

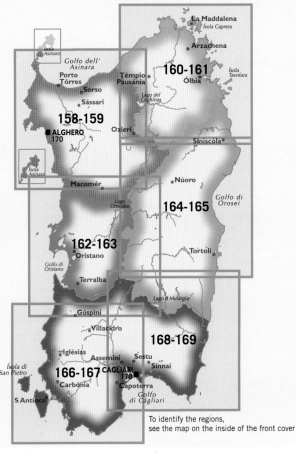

Golfo dell' Asinara
Ísola Asinara
Ísola Asinara
La Maddalena
Ísola Caprera
Arzachena
Porto Tórres
Sorso
Sássari
Témpio Pausánia
Ísola Tavolara
Ólbia
160-161
ALGHERO
170
Ozieri
Siniscóla
Macomér
Lago del Coghinas
Núoro
Golfo di Orosei
Lago Omodeo
158-159
162-163
Oristano
164-165
Tortolí
Golfo di Oristano
Terralba
Lago il Mulárgia
Gúspini
Villacídro
168-169
Iglésias
Assemini
Sestu
Sínnai
Ísola di San Pietro
166-167
CAGLIARI
170
Carbónia
Capoterra
Golfo di Cágliari
S Antioco

To identify the regions,
see the map on the inside of the front cover

Regional Maps

▬▬▬ Major route
▭▭▭ National road
▬▬▬ Regional road
▬▬▬ Other/minor road
▬▬▬ Railway
☐ City
▫ Town/village
✈ Airport
◼ Featured place of interest
◾ Place of interest

158-169 0 ——————— 10 km
         0 ——————— 5 miles

City Plan

～～ Main/other/minor road
▬▬▬ Railway/city wall
◼ Important building
◼ Park/garden
◼ Featured place of interest
ℹ Tourist information
✝ Church
✉ Post Office

170
Cagliari 0 ——————— 400 metres
          0 ——————— 400 yards

170
Alghero   0 ——————— 150 metres
          0 ——————— 150 yards

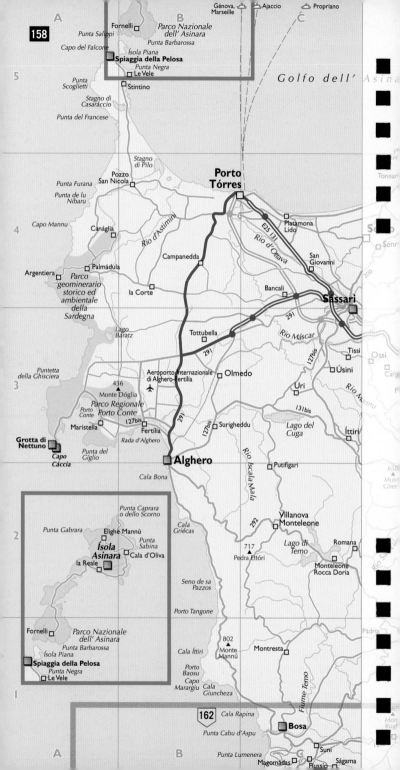

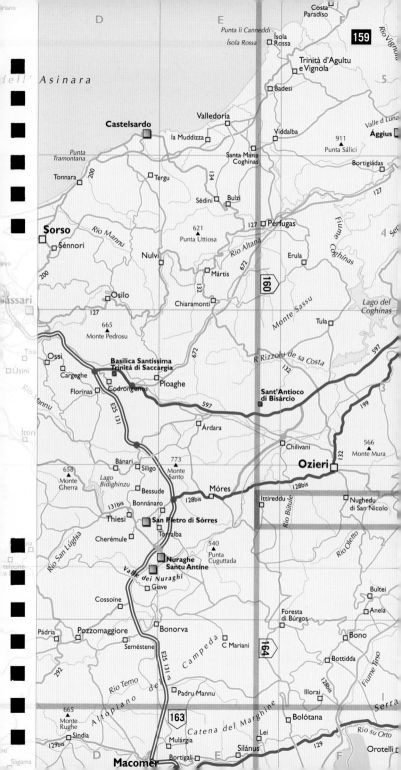

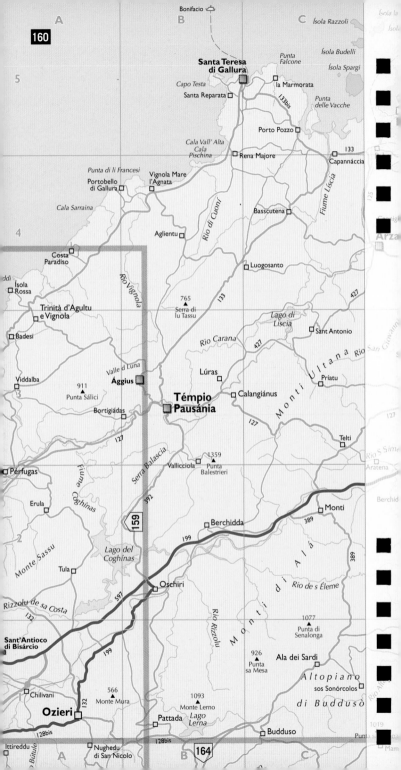

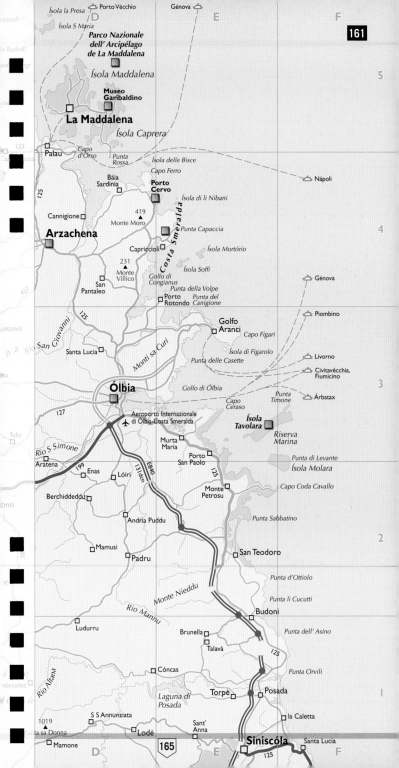

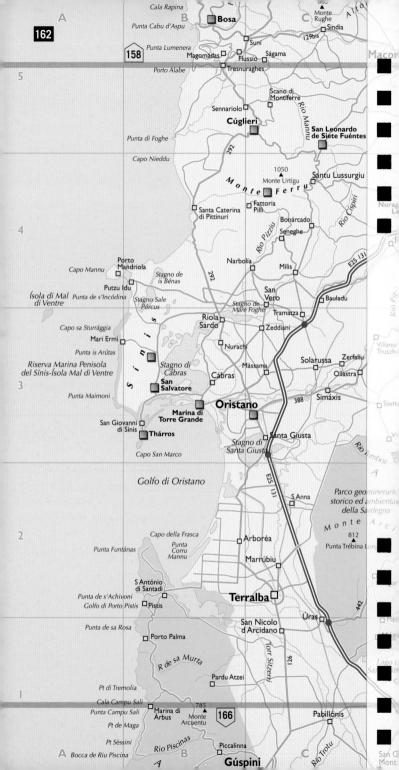

158
166

Bosa
Cala Rapina
Punta Cabu d'Aspu
Punta Lumenera
Porto Alabe
Suni
Magomádas
Flussio
Ságama
Tresnuraghes
Sindia
129bis
Monte
Rughe

Scano di
Montiferre
Sennariolo
Cúglieri
**San Leonardo
de Siète Fuéntes**
Punta di Foghe
292
Rio Mannu

Capo Nieddu
1050
Monte Urtigu
Monte Ferru
Santu Lussurgiu
Fattoria
Pilli
Santa Caterina
di Pittinuri
Bonárcado
Rio Císpiri
Seneghe
Rio Pízzu
Narbolía
Mílis
Capo Mannu
Porto
Mandriola
Ísola di Mal
di Ventre
Punta de s'Incódina
Putzu Idu
Stagno de
is Bénas
292
San
Vero
Bauládu
E25 131
Stagno Sale
Pórcus
Stagno de
Mare Foghe
Tramatza
Capo sa Sturrággia
Mari Ermi
Riola
Sardo
Zeddiani
Punta is Arútas
Nurachi
Riserva Marina Penisola
del Sínis-Ísola Mal di Ventre
Sínis
Stagno di
Cábras
**San
Salvatore**
Mássama
Solarussa
Zerfaliu
Villano
Truschi
Cábras
Ollastra
Siama
Punta Maimoni
388
Simáxis
San Giovanni
di Sínis
**Marina di
Torre Grande**
Oristano
Thárros
Santa Giusta
Capo San Marco
Stagno di
Santa Giusta
Golfo di Oristano
E25
131
S Anna
Parco geo minerario
storico ed ambienta
della Sardegna
Capo della Frasca
Punta
Corru
Mannu
Arboréa
Monte Arci
812
Punta Trébina Lon
Punta Funtánas
Marrúbiu
S António
di Santadi
Punta de s'Achivoni
Golfo di Porto Pistis
Pistis
Terralba
Punta de sa Rosa
San Nicolo
d'Arcidano
Úras
442
Rio Limboi
Lago di
San
Porto Palma
126
Torr Silzerru
Pt di Tremolia
Cala Campu Sali
Punta Campu Sali
Pardu Atzei
**Marina di
Arbus**
785
Monte
Arcuentu
Pabillónis
Pt de Maga
Rio Piscinas
Piccalinna
Pt Sèssini
Bocca de Riu Piscina
Gúspini
Rio Trotu
San D
Mont
Macor

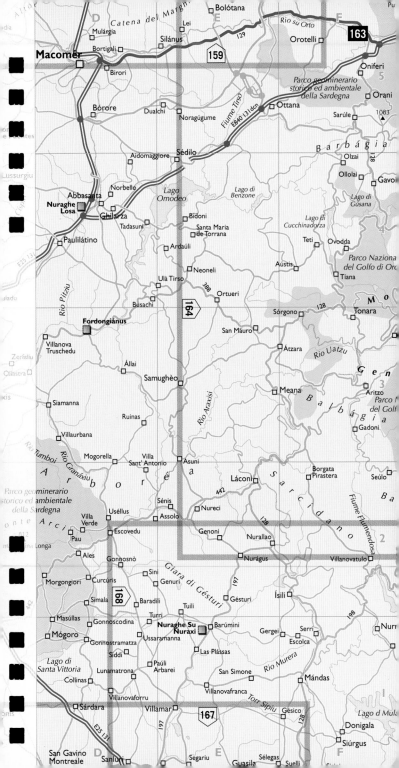

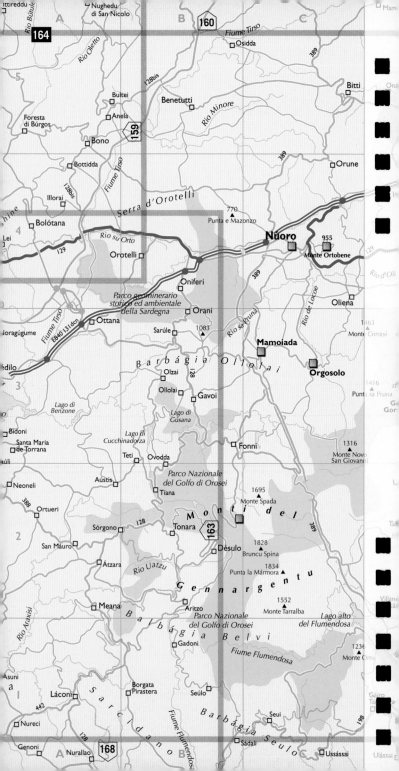

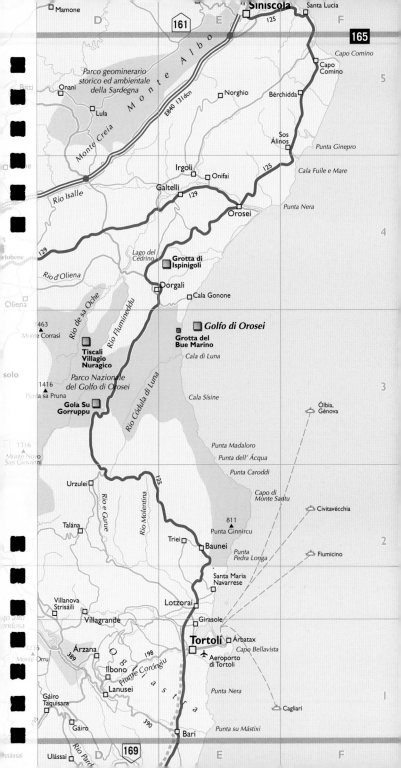

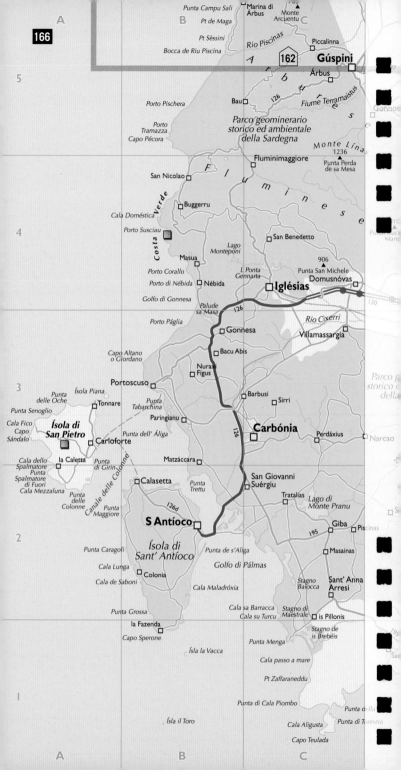

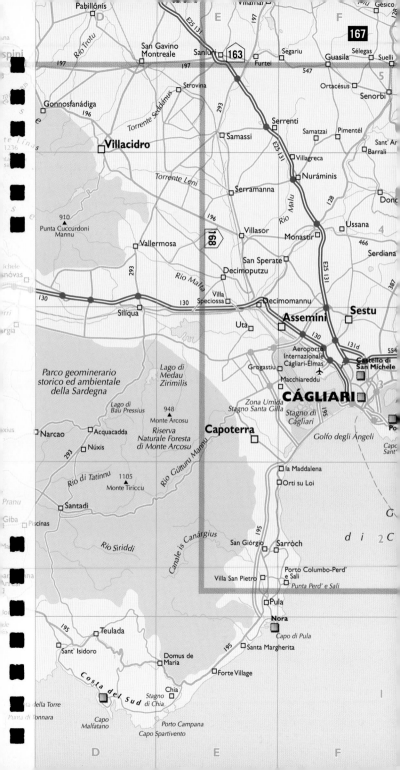

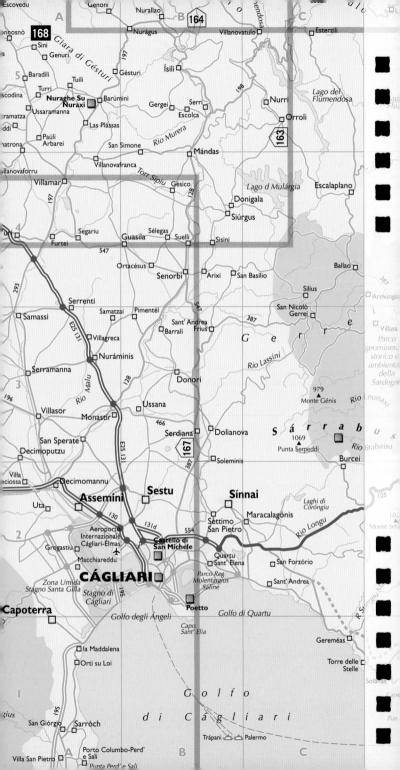

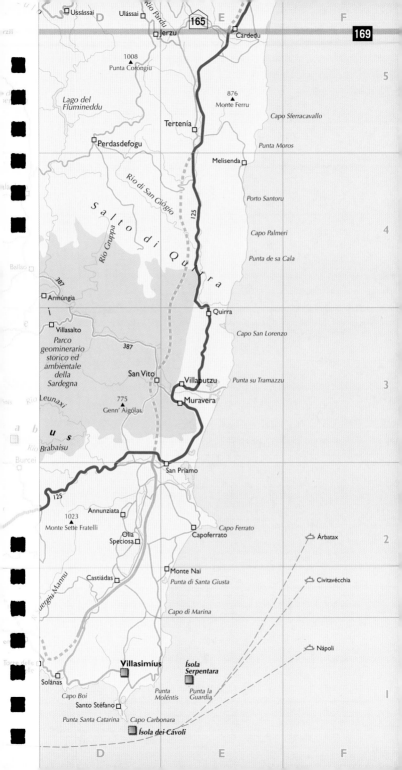

D E F

5

Ussássai
Ulássai
Jerzu
Cardedu

1008
Punta Corongiu

Lago del
Flumineddu

876
Monte Ferru

Capo Sferravallo

Tertenía

Perdasdefogu

Punta Moros

Melisenda

Rio di San Giórgio

Porto Santoru

S a l t o   d i   Q u i r r a

Capo Palmeri

4

Rio Gruppa

125

Punta de sa Cala

Bailao

387

Armúngia

Quirra

Capo San Lorenzo

Villasalto
Parco
geominerario
storico ed
ambientale
della
Sardegna

387

San Vito

Villaputzu

Punta su Tramazzu

3

Leunaxi

775
Genn' Aigólas

Muravera

Rio Brabaisu

u   s

San Priamo

125

Annunziata

1023
Monte Sette Fratelli

Olia
Speciosa

Capoferrato

Capo Ferrato

Árbatax

2

Castiádas

Monte Nai

Punta di Santa Giusta

Civitavécchia

Capo di Marina

Nápoli

Villasimíus

Ísola
Serpentara

1

Solánas

Capo Boi
Santo Stéfano

Punta
Moléntis

Punta la
Guardia

Punta Santa Catarina

Capo Carbonara

Ísola dei Cávoli

D E F

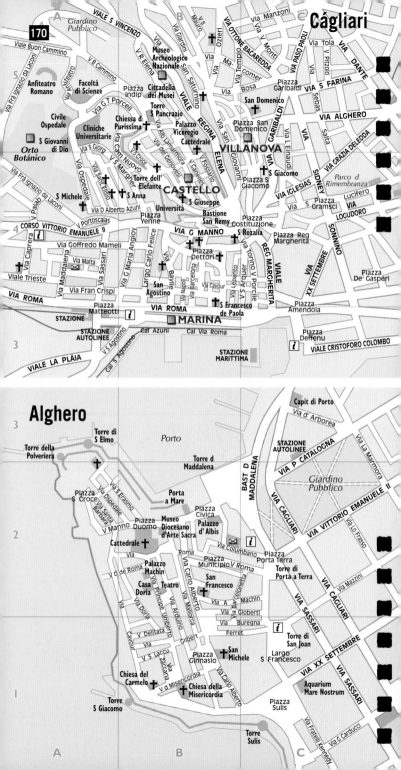

Picture credits

The Automobile Association would like to thank the following photographers, companies and picture libraries for their assistance in the preparation of this book.
Abbreviations for the picture credits are as follows – (t) top; (b) bottom; (c) centre; (l) left; (r) right; (b/g) background; (AA) AA World Travel Library.

Front and back cover images: **(t)** Chiesa di Sant'Antonio, Orosei, AA/Neil Setchfield; **(ct)** Arcipélago de La Maddalena, AA/Neil Setchfield; **(c)** Golfo di Orosei, AA/Neil Setchfield; **(b)** Cúglieri, AA/Neil Setchfield
Spine: Nuraghe Santu Antíne, AA/Neil Setchfield

2(i) AA/Neil Setchfield; **2(ii)** AA/Neil Setchfield; **2(iii)** AA/Neil Setchfield; **2(iv)** AA/Neil Setchfield; **2(v)** AA/Neil Setchfield; **3(i)** AA/Neil Setchfield; **3(ii)** AA/Neil Setchfield; **3(iii)** AA/Neil Setchfield; **3(iv)** AA/Clive Sawyer; **5** AA/Neil Setchfield; **6** AA/Neil Setchfield; **7cr** AA/Neil Setchfield; **7b** AA/Neil Setchfield; **8** AA/Neil Setchfield; **9c** AA/Neil Setchfield; **9b** AA/Neil Setchfield; **10** AA/Neil Setchfield; **11 b/g** AA/Clive Sawyer; **11tl** AA/Clive Sawyer; **12** AA/Neil Setchfield; **13t** AA/Neil Setchfield; **13b** AA/Neil Setchfield; **14** David Sutherland/Alamy; **15** SIME/Morandi Bruno/4Corners Images; **16–17 b/g** AA/Neil Setchfield; **16b** AA/Neil Setchfield; **17t** AA/Neil Setchfield; **18b** AA/Neil Setchfield; **19** AA/Neil Setchfield; **20** AA/Neil Setchfield; **22** AA/Neil Setchfield; **23t** SIME/Scatà Stefano/4Corners Images; **23c** AA/Neil Setchfield; **24** Foodfolio/ Pictures Colour Library; **25** John Miller; **26–27** AA/Neil Setchfield; **28** AA/Neil Setchfield; **29t** Dietmar Nill/Nature Picture Library; **29cr** Panda Photo/FLPA; **29cr** AA/Neil Setchfield; **29b** blickwinkel/Alamy; **30** SIME/Ripani Massimo/4Corners Images; **31** AA/Neil Setchfield; **41** AA/Neil Setchfield; **42** AA/Neil Setchfield; **43** AA/Neil Setchfield; **44c** AA/Neil Setchfield; **44b** AA/Neil Setchfield; **45** AA/Neil Setchfield; **46** SIME/Morandi Bruno/4Corners Images; **47** AA/Clive Sawyer; **48** AA/Neil Setchfield; **49** AA/Neil Setchfield; **50** AA/Neil Setchfield; **51c** AA/Neil Setchfield; **51b** AA/Neil Setchfield; **52** AA/Neil Setchfield; **53** AA/Neil Setchfield; **54l** AA/Neil Setchfield; **54–55b** SIME/Spila Riccardo/4Corners Images; **55br** AA/Neil Setchfield; **56–88** AA/Neil Setchfield; **89** SIME/Ripani Massimo/4Corners Images; **90** CuboImages srl/Alamy; **91–118** AA/Neil Setchfield; **119** AA/Clive Sawyer; **120c** AA/Neil Setchfield; **120b** AA/Neil Setchfield; **121–148** AA/Neil Setchfield; **149** AA/Clive Sawyer; **153t** AA/Neil Setchfield; **153cl** AA/Neil Setchfield; **153cr** AA/Neil Setchfield.

Every effort has been made to trace the copyright holders, and we apologise in advance for any accidental errors. We would be happy to apply the correction in the following edition of this publication.

The author would like to thank Alison, Polly and Hugh from Just Sardinia in England for arranging car hire, assistance with accommodation and their boundless enthusiasm. Many thanks also to Martin for his great support, Renata, the Italian Tourist Board in London, Marina Tavolata from Travel Marketing in Rome, Sally and "Sir Rupert".

Questionnaire

Dear Traveller

Your comments, opinions and recommendations
are very important to us. So please help us to improve
our travel guides by taking a few minutes to complete
this simple questionnaire.

You do not need a stamp (unless posted outside the UK). If you do not
want to remove this page from your guide, then photocopy it or write your
answers on a plain sheet of paper.

Send to: The Editor, Spiral Guides, AA World Travel Guides,
FREEPOST SCE 4598, Basingstoke RG21 4GY.

Your recommendations...

We always encourage readers' recommendations for restaurants, night-life or shopping
– if your recommendation is used in the next edition of the guide, we will send you a
FREE AA Spiral Guide of your choice. Please state below the establishment name,
location and your reasons for recommending it.

_____

_____

_____

_____

_____

Please send me AA Spiral _____

(see list of titles inside the back cover)

About this guide...

Which title did you buy?

_____ **AA Spiral**

Where did you buy it? _____

When? m m / y y

Why did you choose an AA Spiral Guide? _____

_____

_____

_____

_____

Did this guide meet your expectations?

Exceeded ☐   Met all ☐   Met most ☐   Fell below ☐

Please give your reasons _____

_____

_____

_____

_____

continued on next page...

Were there any aspects of this guide that you particularly liked?

_____

_____

_____

_____

_____

Is there anything we could have done better?

_____

_____

_____

_____

About you...

Name (Mr/Mrs/Ms) _____

Address _____

_____

_____ **Postcode** _____

Daytime tel no _____ **email** _____

Please _only_ give us your email address and mobile phone number if you wish to hear from us about other products and services from the AA and partners by email or text or mms.

Which age group are you in?

Under 25 ☐   25–34 ☐   35–44 ☐   45–54 ☐   55–64 ☐   65+ ☐

How many trips do you make a year?

Less than one ☐   One ☐   Two ☐   Three or more ☐

Are you an AA member? Yes ☐   No ☐

About your trip...

When did you book? mm/ y y   **When did you travel?** mm/ y y

How long did you stay? _____

Was it for business or leisure? _____

Did you buy any other travel guides for your trip? ☐ Yes   ☐ No

If yes, which ones? _____

_____

Thank you for taking the time to complete this questionnaire. Please send it to us as soon as possible, and remember, you do not need a stamp (unless posted outside the UK).